THE COMPLETE
PRO TOOLS
SHORTCUTS

By José "Chilitos" Valenzuela

Backbeat
Books
San Francisco

Published by Backbeat Books
600 Harrison Street, San Francisco, CA 94107
www.backbeatbooks.com
email: books@musicplayer.com

An imprint of CMP Information
Publishers of *Guitar Player*, *Bass Player*, *Keyboard*, and *EQ* magazines

CMP
United Business Media

Distributed to the book trade in the US and Canada by
Publishers Group West, 1700 Fourth Street, Berkeley, CA 94710

Distributed to the music trade in the US and Canada by
Hal Leonard Publishing, P.O. Box 13819, Milwaukee, WI 53213

Graphic design and editing: Ana Lorente Izquierdo
Cover design: Damien Castaneda
Front and back cover photo: Oscar Elizondo
Photographer assistant: Julian Salas
Editors: George Madaraz and Karl Coryat
Technical editors: Neal Kiyoshi Fujio and Gary Glass
Proofreaders: Andre Oliveira, Roberto C. González Fócil, Gary Glass, Don Q. Hannah,
        Vivian Khor, Neal Kiyoshi Fujio, Giovanna Imbesi, Jamie Steele

Library of Congress Cataloging-in-Publication Data

Valenzuela, José.
The complete Pro Tools shortcuts / by José "Chilitos" Valenzuela.
    p. cm.
Includes bibliographical references.
ISBN 0-87930-807-9 (alk. paper)
1. Pro Tools. 2. Digital audio editors. I. Title.

TK7881.4.V3523 2004
621.389'3'0285536—dc22

                    2004023443

Printed in the United States of America

04 05 06 07 08   5 4 3 2 1

Please send all suggestions and questions
to the author at the following address:

AudioGraph International
Attn: José "Chilitos" Valenzuela
2103 Main Street
Santa Monica, CA 90405, USA
Tel: (310) 396-5004 • Fax: (310) 396-5882
E-mail: chilitos@audiographintl.com

Table of Contents

Dedication

I dedicate this book to two very special people who recognized and embraced my talent early on, believing in the heights of human potential when given opportunity.

Thank you Doctor for seeing me as you always knew I could be and giving me the opportunity to be the person that I am today.

In Loving Memory,

Mr. Ronald A. Cummings, M.D.

and

Mrs. Adalene S. Cummings

Introduction

You may be wondering how the idea of publishing a Pro Tools Shortcuts book like the one you are holding in your hands right now came about. Well, it's very simple. I decided to publish a book of this nature because the first time I worked on a high-profile job using Pro Tools in a studio—twelve years ago—I was asked by the producer to apply a crossfade between two audio regions on a track. At that time, I was not sure where the Fades command was in order to create the crossfade so I started to scan nervously through the drop-down menus with an uncertain look on my face. Consequently, he began to question if I knew what I was doing and did not hire me back again, which taught me an important lesson: I should have memorized and used the shortcuts while using Pro Tools because I would have looked cooler and more professional.

There is quite a bit of helpful information in this shortcuts book that, with all the screenshots included, you should not have any problems understanding and applying. I highly recommend that you learn and memorize them because they will help you to be a successful Pro Tools engineer/editor. Please enjoy the book and have lots of fun using what you learn.

Chilitos
www.audiographintl.com

How To Use This Book

The shortcuts are listed first for Macintosh and then for PC. Also, notice there is a picture of a keyboard with the keys that should be pressed shaded in black to make the key commands easier to read.

Whenever you find more than one picture to explain a shortcut, keep in mind that these follow a certain order. The picture closest to the left side of the page shows what you should see before applying the shortcut, and the picture closest to the right side of the page shows what you should see after applying the shortcut. In a few instances you will see three pictures to describe the shortcut, the first picture being what you see before applying the shortcut, the second, what you see after applying it but before it is completed, and the third will be the result of applying it.

Not all the shortcuts are easy to explain on paper, so it is always a good idea to practice with Pro Tools while referencing these pages. Some of them will be much easier to remember and understand if you see the results on your screen.

Pro Tools Keyboard Stickers

Enter Start End / Length	Enter, Start, End, Length
Capture (=)	Capture Time Code
F12 (R)	Record
F11	Wait for Note
F10	Pencil Tool
F9	Scrubber Tools
F8	Grabber Tools
F7	Selector Tool
F6	Trimmer Tools
F5	Zoomer Tool
F4 Grid	Grid Mode
F3 Spot	Spot Mode
F2 Slip	Slip Mode
F1 Shuffle	Shuffle Mode

−	Nudge Back
Enter Main Counter *	Enter Main Counter
Capture (+ =)	Capture Time Code
−	Track View Toggle
) 0	Edit Sel to TL Sel
(9	Play From Edit End
* 8	Play To Edit End
& 7	Play From Edit Start
^ 6	Play To Edit Start
% 5	Zoom 5
$ 4	Zoom 4
# 3	Zoom 3
@ 2	Zoom 2
! 1	Zoom 1

enter	Create Mem Loc
+	Nudge Forward
1	Play TL Sel
I	Play Edit Sel
P	Move Edit Sel Up
O	TL Sel to Edit Sel
I	Snap End to TC
U	Snap Sync to TC
Y	Snap Start to TC
T	Zoom in Horizontal
R	Zoom Out Horizontal
E	Zoom Toggle
W	Center TL End
Q	Center TL Start

.	Recall Mem Loc
9	Merge/Replace
BLANK	
	Next Start/End
	Move Edit Sel Down
L	Previous Start/End
K	Snap End to Play
J	Snap Sync to Play
H	Snap Start to Play
G	Fade To End
F	Crossfade
D	Fade From Start
S	Trim End
A	Trim Start

8	Countoff
7	Metronome
BLANK	
Space Bar	Play/Stop
? /	Nudge Fwd
>	Nudge Forward
<	Nudge Back
M	Nudge Back
N	Insertion Follows PB
B	Separate
V	Paste
C	Copy
X	Cut
Z	Undo

6	QuickPunch
5	Loop Record
4	Loop Playback
3 (R)	Record
2	Fast Forward
1	Rewind
0	Play/Stop
BLANK	
BLANK	
BLANK	
	Center Edit End
	Center Edit Start
	Mark Edit End
	Mark Edit Start

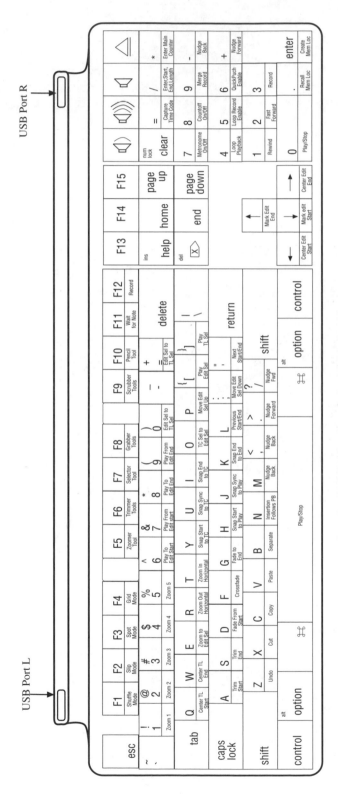

Apple USB Keyboard (108 key)

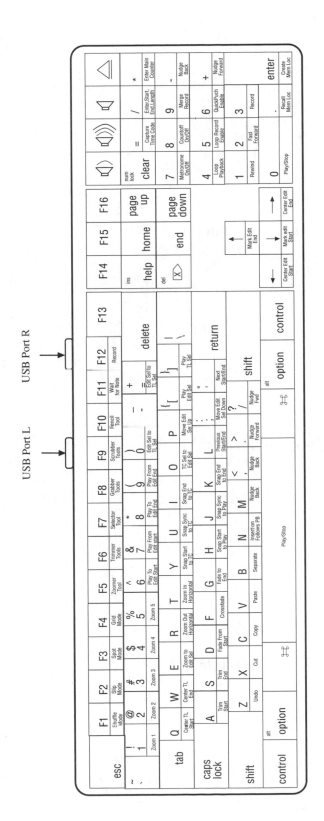

Apple USB Keyboard (109 key)

Function Keys

(Alpha) means that you must press the number on the main section of the computer keyboard, i.e., the alphanumeric section of the keyboard, not the numeric keypad on the right of the keyboard.

Shuffle Mode →

Option + 1 (Alpha*) or F1
PC: F1

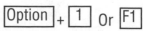

If you decided to use "Hot Keys" then you must hold down the Option key and click on the Function key, ex: F1.

Slip Mode →

Option + 2 (Alpha*) or F2
PC: F2

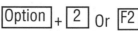

Spot Mode →

Option + 3 (Alpha*) or F3
PC: F3

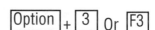

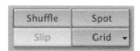

Grid Mode →

Option + 4 (Alpha*) or F4
PC: F4

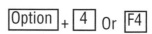

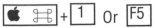

Command + 1 (Alpha*) or F5
PC: Ctrl + 1 (Alpha) or F5

← <u>**Zoomer Tool**</u>

Command + 2 (Alpha*) or F6
PC: Ctrl + 2 (Alpha*) or F6

← <u>**Trimmer Tool**</u>

Trimmer Tool options:
1) Standard
2) Scrub (TDM systems only)
3) TCE (Time Compression/Expansion)

Command + 3 (Alpha*) or F7
PC: Ctrl + 3 (Alpha*) or F7

← <u>**Selector Tool**</u>

Command + 4 (Alpha*) or F8
PC: Ctrl + 4 (Alpha*) or F8

← <u>**Grabber Tool**</u>

Grabber Tool options:
1) Time
2) Separation
3) Object (TDM systems only)

Scrubber Tool →

Command + 5 (Alpha*) or F9
PC: Ctrl + 5 (Alpha*) or F9

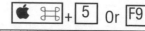

Pencil Tool →

Different functions of the Pencil Tool:
- *Freehand*
- *Line*
- *Triangle*
- *Square*
- *Random*

Command + 6 (Alpha*) or F10
PC: Ctrl + 6 (Alpha*) or F10

NOTE: If you keep pressing the number key over and over again, the pencil tool options will cycle through.

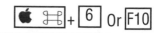

Smart Tool →

Command + 7 (Alpha*), or F6 & F7, or F7 & F8
PC: Ctrl + 7 (Alpha*), or F6 & F7, or F7 & F8

Cycle through Edit Tools →

Escape Key
PC: Center Mouse Click

Cycle through Edit Modes →

"~" Key
PC: "~" Key

RECORD AND PLAYBACK OPTIONS

Return
PC: Enter

←Go to Start of Session

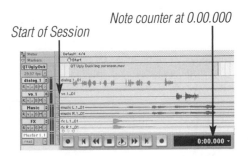

Note counter at 0.00.000

Start of Session

Option + Return
PC: Alt + Enter

←Go to End of Session

End of Session

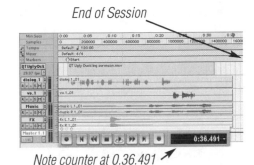

Note counter at 0.36.491

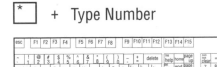

* (Numeric *) and typing a number of the desired location and then press the Return or Enter key

←Enter Cursor Location

[*] + Type Number

*(Numeric *) means the number must be pressed from the numeric keypad of the computer keyboard (right side of the keyboard).*

—*Numeric Keypad*

Note that the counter is highlighted

Spacebar or Ø (Numeric *)
PC: Spacebar or Ø (Numeric *)

←Playback/Stop

Stop button

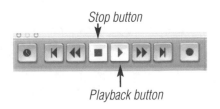

Playback button

— *Numeric Keypad*

Half-Speed Playback →

Shift + Spacebar

PC: Shift + Spacebar

Rewind →

1 (Numeric *)

PC: 1 (Numeric)

*NOTE: The "Numeric Keypad mode"
located in the "Setups > Preferences >
Operation" menu should be assigned to
"Transport."*

Fast Forward →

2 (Numeric *)

PC: 2 (Numeric)

*NOTE: The "Numeric Keypad mode"
located in the "Setups > Preferences >
Operation" menu should be assigned to
"Transport."*

Loop Playback →

4 (Numeric *) or Shift + Command + L or hold down the Control key
and click on the Play button in the Transport window

PC: 4 (Numeric)

*NOTE: You must have a region
selected for the "Loop Playback"
function to take effect.*

4

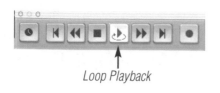

Loop Playback

3 (Numeric *) or Command + Spacebar or F12 ← **Record**
PC: Ctrl + Spacebar or F12 or 3 (Numeric)

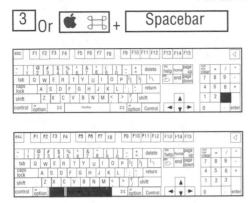

Record and Playback buttons

Shift + Command + Spacebar ← **Half-Speed Record**
PC: Shift + Ctrl + Spacebar

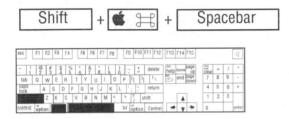

5 (Numeric *) or Option + L or hold down the Control key ← **Loop Record**
and click on the Record button in the Transport window **Enable/Disable**
PC: 5 (Numeric *)

NOTE: To select the Loop Record function through the Transport window, keep clicking the Record button while holding down the Control key until you see a red circle around it.

Loop Record mode enabled

6 (Numeric *) or Shift + Command + P or hold down the Con- ← **Quick Punch**
trol key and click on the Record button in the Transport window **Enable/Disable**
PC: 6 (Numeric *)

NOTE: To select the Quick Punch function through the Transport window, keep clicking the Record button while holding down the Control key until you see the letter "P" in it.

Note the "P" inside the Record button

Metronome On/Off →

7 (Numeric *)
PC: 7 (Numeric *)

Metronome button enabled

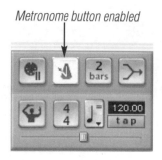

Count On/Off →

8 (Numeric *)
PC: 8 (Numeric *)

Count On/Off button enabled

Merge Record →

9 (Numeric *)
PC: 9 (Numeric *)

Merge Record button enabled

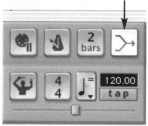

Stop Record and Discard Take →

Command + "." (Numeric *)
PC: Esc or Ctrl + "." (Numeric *)

After applying the shortcut, the recording process was stopped and the take was discarded. Also, notice the existing region was not over-written.

Recording audio over an existing region

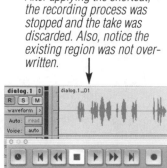

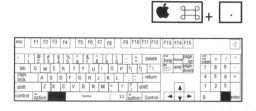

Control + Spacebar or Option + Command + Click on Play button
PC: Alt + Start + Spacebar + Click on Play button or Spacebar

← **Pause (for instant Playback)**

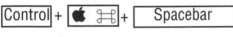

NOTE: Notice the Stop button is lit solid and the Play button in the Transport window is flashing.

Play button in the Transport window is flashing

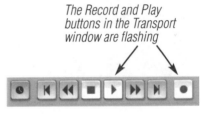

Control + Command + Click on Spacebar
PC: Alt + Start + Click on Record button

← **Pause (for instant Record)**

NOTE: You must have an audio or MIDI track record enabled. Notice the Stop button is lit solid and the Play and Record buttons in the Transport window start flashing.

The Record and Play buttons in the Transport window are flashing

Command + J
PC: Ctrl + J

← **Online/Offline**

The Online button in the Transport window is flashing

NOTE: Notice the Clock icon button in the Transport window starts flashing.

Shift + Command + J

←**Movie Online**

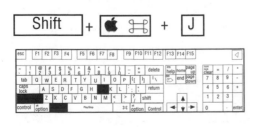

NOTE: You must have a QuickTime movie in your Pro Tools session for this shortcut to function.

11

Enable/Disable Online Record→

Option + Command + Spacebar
PC: Ctrl + Alt + Spacebar

NOTE: An audio or MIDI track must be record-enabled in your session.

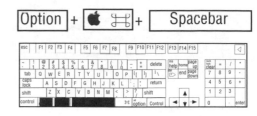

Enable/Disable Online Playback→

Option + Spacebar or Command + J
PC: Ctrl + J or Alt + Spacebar

NOTE: In order to start playback, a time code signal must be present.

Toggle Record Modes:→
Normal/Destructive/
Loop/QuickPunch

Control + Click on Record button in Transport window
PC: Right Mouse Click on Record button in Transport window

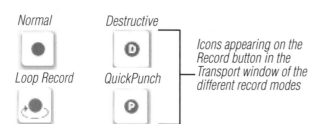

Normal *Destructive*

Loop Record *QuickPunch*

Icons appearing on the Record button in the Transport window of the different record modes

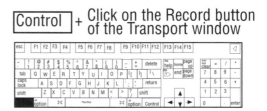

Loop Playback Toggle→

Shift + Command + L or Control + Cilck on Play button
PC: Start + Click or Right Mouse Click on Play button

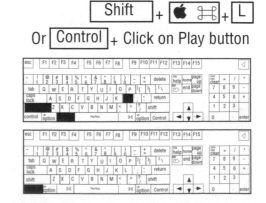

Command + Click on "Record Enable" button ◄—**Record Safe Track**
PC: Ctrl + Click on "Record Enable" button

 + Click on "Record Enable" Button

Notice that the Record Enable button looks greyed out

NOTE: This is so you won't set an already recorded track into record mode, erasing what you already have in it.

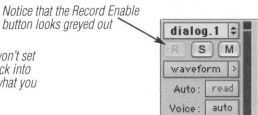

Command + Click on Solo button ◄—**Solo-Safe Track**
PC: Ctrl + Click on Solo button

 + Click on Solo Button

NOTE: This is so the track you "Solo safe" won't be affected when you Solo another track. In other words, it will still play back even if another track is set to solo.

Notice that the Solo button looks greyed out

Shift + Command + P ◄—**Quick Punch Recording Enable/Disable**
PC: Ctrl + Shift + P

Shift +  + P

Command + Spacebar or
Command + Click on Record button ◄—**Enter/Exit Record during Playback in Quick Punch**
PC: Ctrl + Spacebar or Ctrl + Click on Record button

 + Spacebar Or

 + Click on Record button

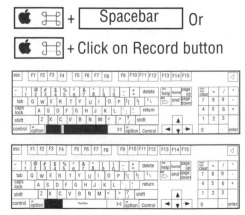

Enter Record   *Exit Record*

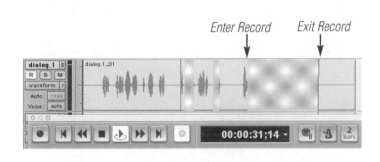

Pre- & Post-roll Time Enable/Disable →

Command + K
PC: Ctrl + K

Pre- & Post-roll time buttons are enabled when they are highlighted

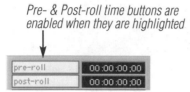

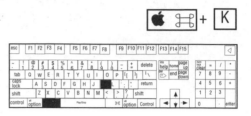

Pre-roll Time Set and Enable → Option + Click with the Selector Tool before the selection
PC: Alt + Click with Selector Tool before the selection

Option + Click with Selector before the selection

Pre-roll time

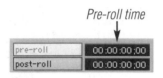

NOTE: You must position the Selector tool to where you want the playback or the recording to start, then press the Option key and click anywhere to the left of your selection. You will notice the Pre-roll button on the Transport window will be highlighted and a Pre-roll time will be set as well. Try it!

Post-roll Time Set and Enable →

Option + Click with the Selector Tool after the selection
PC: Alt + click with Selector Tool after the selection

Option + Click with Selector after the selection

NOTE: Same as above but this time you have to click to the right of your selection.

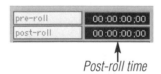

Post-roll time

Pre-roll Time Disable →

Option + Click within selection closer to the start point
PC: Alt + Click within selection closer to the start point

Option + Click within selection closer to the start point

NOTE: A selection must be made in order to click inside closer to the start point of the selection.

Option + Click within selection closer to the end point ◄── **Post-roll Time Disable**

PC: Alt + Click within selection closer to the end point

 + Click within selection closer to the end point

NOTE: A selection must be made in order to click inside closer to the end point of the selection.

Command + \ ◄── **Toggle Transport Master**

**PC: Ctrl + **

(Pro Tools/Machine/MMC)

 + \

NOTE: You must have "Machine" or "MIDI Machine Control" enabled in the Peripherals menu in order to achieve this.

VIEW OPTIONS

<u>Zoom In</u>→

Select the Zoomer Tool and Click on the waveform
PC: Select the Zoomer Tool and Click on the waveform

Notice the region in the second track was zoomed in.

←——— *Second track* ———→

<u>Zoom Out</u>→

Option + Click on the waveform with the Zoomer Tool
PC: Alt + Click on the waveform with the Zoomer Tool

| Option | + Click on the waveform

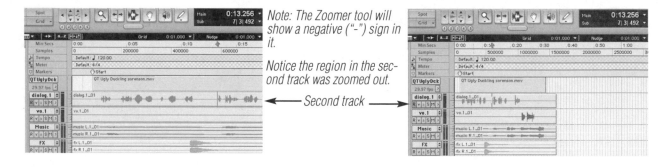

Note: The Zoomer tool will show a negative ("-") sign in it.

Notice the region in the second track was zoomed out.

←——— *Second track* ———→

<u>View Entire Session</u>→

Option + A or Double-Click on the Zoomer Tool
PC: Alt + A or Double-Click on the Zoomer Tool

The entire region's length is shown.

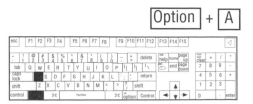

| Option | + | A |

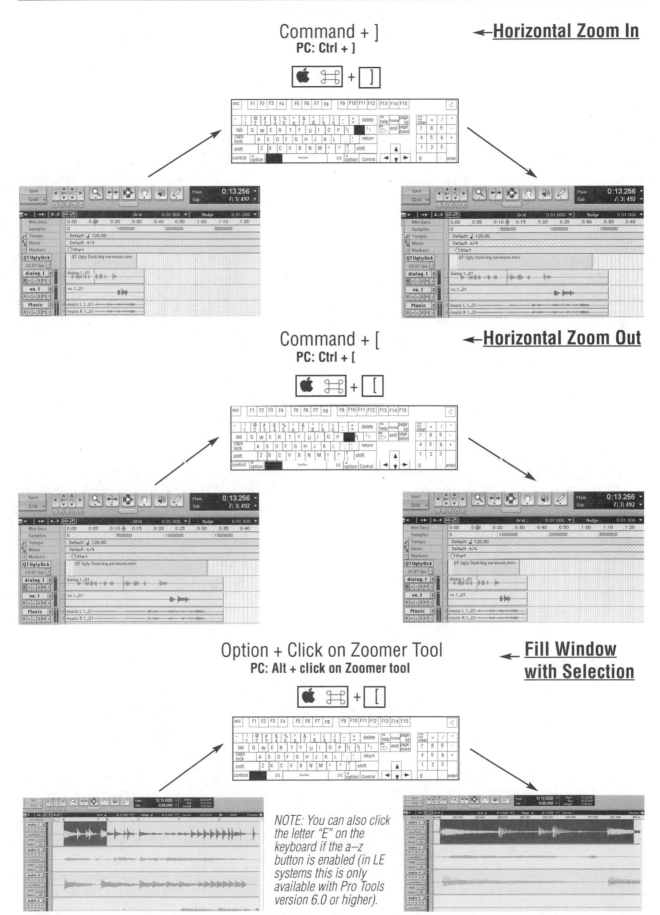

Command +]
PC: Ctrl +]

←**Horizontal Zoom In**

Command + [
PC: Ctrl + [

←**Horizontal Zoom Out**

Option + Click on Zoomer Tool
PC: Alt + click on Zoomer tool

← **Fill Window
with Selection**

NOTE: You can also click the letter "E" on the keyboard if the a–z button is enabled (in LE systems this is only available with Pro Tools version 6.0 or higher).

Vertical Zoom In (Audio) → Option + Command +]
PC: Ctrl + Alt +]

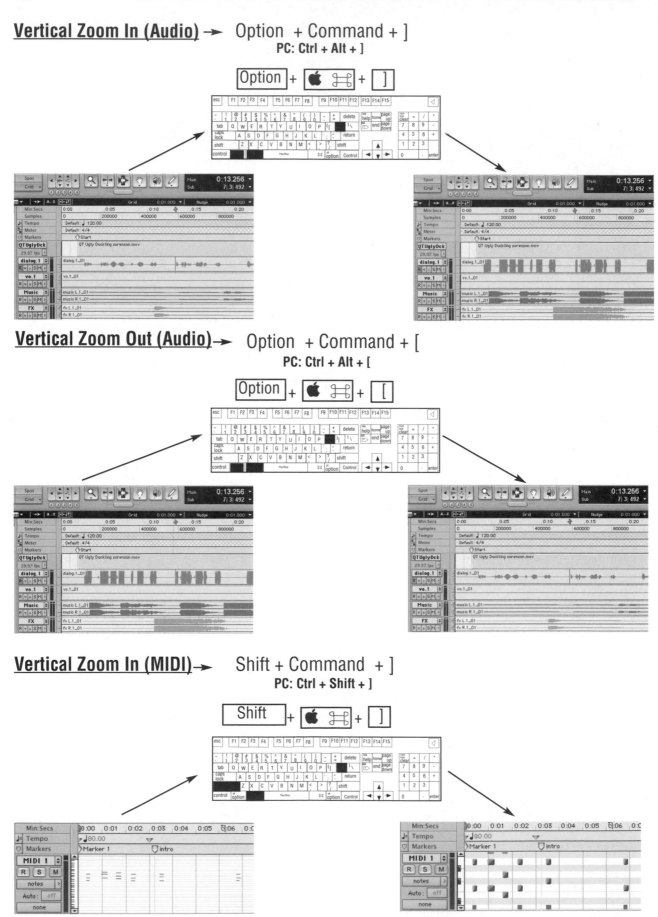

Vertical Zoom Out (Audio) → Option + Command + [
PC: Ctrl + Alt + [

Vertical Zoom In (MIDI) → Shift + Command +]
PC: Ctrl + Shift +]

Shift + Command + [← **Vertical Zoom Out (MIDI)**
PC: Ctrl + Shift + [

Shift + 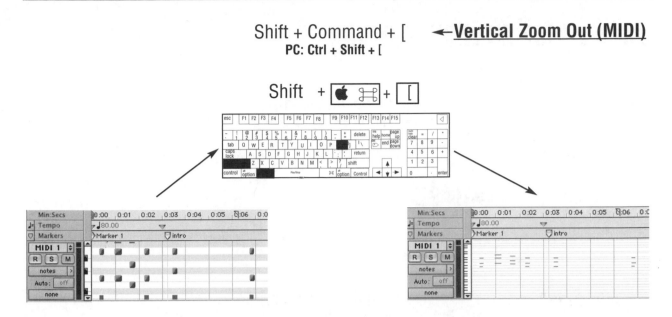 + [

1 Through 5 (Alpha *) ← **Select Preset Zoom Settings**
PC: 1 through 5 (Alpha *)

Zoom Preset buttons

Command + Click on desired Zoom preset button
(it will blink several times to indicate the new setting has been stored)

→ **To Store Your Own Preset Zoom Settings**

PC: Ctrl + Click on desired Zoom preset button
(it will blink several times to indicate the new setting has been stored)

 + Click on any Zoom preset button

Zoom preset buttons

SHOW/HIDE WINDOW OPTIONS

<u>Transport</u> →

Command + 1 (Numeric *)
PC: Ctrl + 1 (Numeric *)

Session Setup window

<u>Session Setup</u> →

Command + 2 (Numeric *)
PC: Ctrl + 2 (Numeric *)

Session Setup window

<u>Big Counter</u> →

Command + 3 (Numeric *)
PC: Ctrl + 3 (Numeric *)

Big Counter window

<u>Automation Enable</u> →

Command + 4 (Numeric *)
PC: Ctrl + 4 (Numeric *)

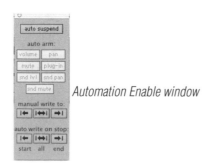

Automation Enable window

Command + 5 (Numeric *)
PC: Ctrl + 5 (Numeric *)

←**Memory Locations**

Memory Locations window

Command + 6 (Numeric *)
PC: Ctrl + 6 (Numeric *)

←**Machine Track Arm**
(TDM systems only)

Command + 7 (Numeric *)
PC: Ctrl + 7 (Numeric *)

←**Show Universe**
(TDM systems only)

Universe window

Command + 8 (Numeric *)
PC: Ctrl + 8 (Numeric *)

←**Beat Detective**
(TDM systems only)

Beat Detective window

Movie →

Command + 9 (Numeric *)
PC: Ctrl + 9 (Numeric *)

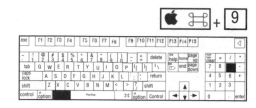

Movie window

NOTE: A QuickTime movie must be present in the Pro Tools session.

MIDI Event List →

Option + Equal "=" (Numeric *)
PC: Alt + Equal "=" (Numeric *)

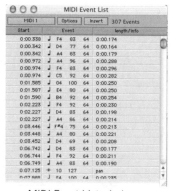

MIDI Event List window

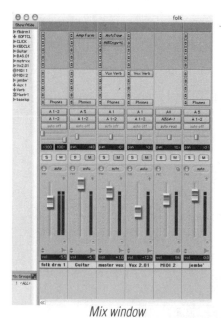

Mix →

Command + Equal "=" (Alpha *)
PC: Ctrl + Equal "=" (Alpha *)

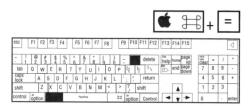

Mix window

Command + U
PC: Ctrl + U

 +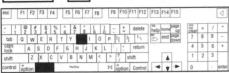

←**Strip Silence**

Strip Silence window

GENERAL OPTIONS

Create New Session →

Command + N
PC: Ctrl + N

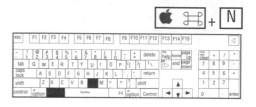

Open Session →

Command + O
PC: Ctrl + O

Close Session →

Command + W (Once to hide Mix or Edit
window, second time to close session)
PC: Ctrl + Shift + W (Once to hide Mix or Edit
window, second time to close session)

Save Session →

Command + S
PC: Ctrl + S

Command + Q   ←**Quit Pro Tools**

Shift + Command + N   ←**New Track**
PC: Ctrl + Shift + N

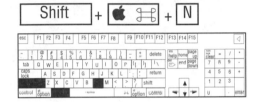

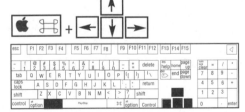

Command + Up/Down/Left/Right arrows ←**Cycle through New Track Options**
PC: Ctrl + Up/Down/Left/Right arrows

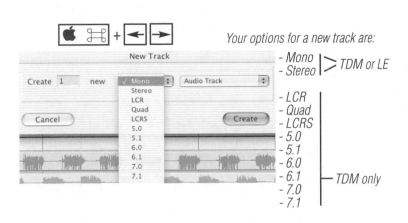

Your options for a new track are:

- Mono
- Stereo } TDM or LE

- LCR
- Quad
- LCRS
- 5.0
- 5.1
- 6.0
- 6.1
- 7.0
- 7.1

— TDM only

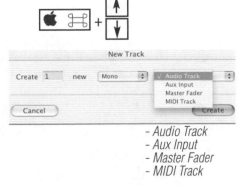

- Audio Track
- Aux Input
- Master Fader
- MIDI Track

25

EDIT OPTIONS

Cut →

Command + X
PC: Ctrl + X

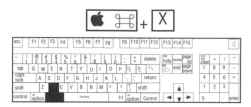

Cut region

Copy →

Command + C
PC: Ctrl + C

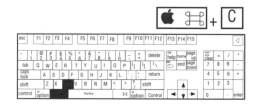

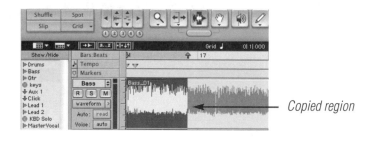

Copied region

Paste →

Command + V
PC: Ctrl + V

Before applying the Paste shortcut place the cursor wherever you want the copied region to be pasted.

Pasted region

Command + Z
PC: Ctrl + Z

←<u>**Undo**</u>

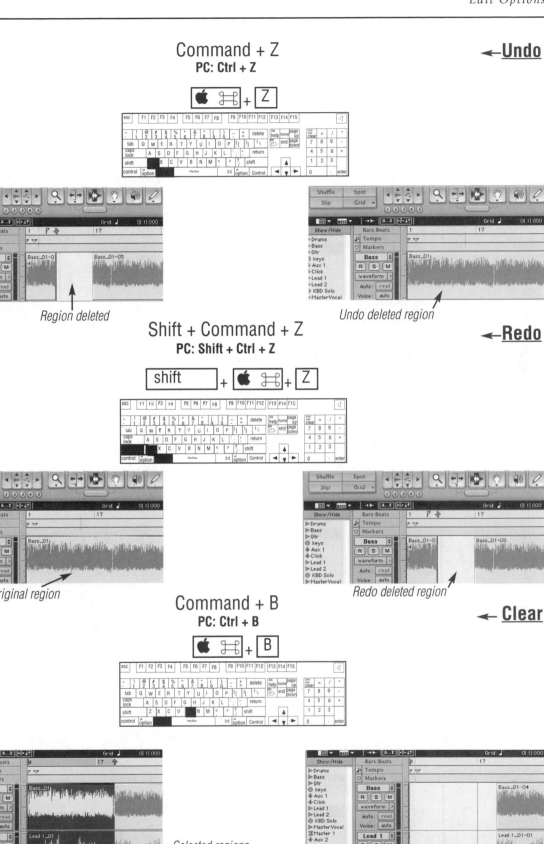

Region deleted

Undo deleted region

Shift + Command + Z
PC: Shift + Ctrl + Z

←<u>**Redo**</u>

Original region

Redo deleted region

Command + B
PC: Ctrl + B

← <u>**Clear**</u>

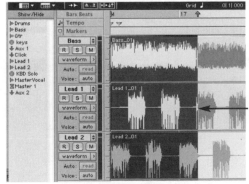

Selected regions to be cleared

Cleared regions

Mute Selected Region →　Command + M
PC: Ctrl + M

Region selected to be muted

NOTE: Notice the selected region gets greyed out (muted).

Region muted (greyed out)

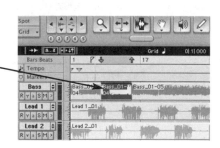

Duplicate Selected Region →　Command + D
PC: Ctrl + D

The region selected will be the region duplicated.

Region selected

Region duplicated. Notice the name of the new region.

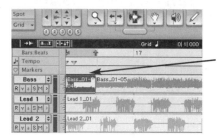

Duplicate Selected Tracks →　Shift + Option + D
PC: Shift + Alt + D

NOTE: Notice that in the picture on the left side two tracks are selected. In the picture on the right, the two tracks were duplicated (highlighted).

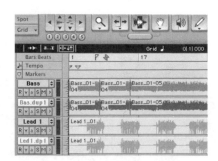

Option + R
PC: Alt + R

 ← **Repeat Selected Region**

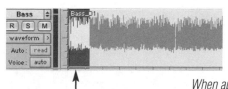

Region selected

When applying this shortcut a Dialog Box will prompt you for the number of repeats you wish to create.

Regions repeated

Option + H
PC: Alt + H

← **Shift Selected Region**

NOTE: You can shift the region "Earlier" or "Later."

Option + M
PC: Alt + M

← **Merge Paste**

(MIDI only)

NOTE: First, you must have copied a selection of MIDI notes in order to use "Merge Paste."

Capture Region →

Command + R
PC: Ctrl + R

The new captured region has been dragged and placed in a new audio track from the Audio Regions List.

When applying this shortcut, a dialog box will prompt you to name the selected region to be captured.

Selected region

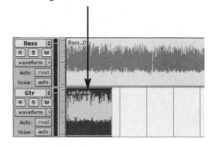

Separate Region →

Command + E
PC: Ctrl + E

Selected region

When applying this shortcut, a dialog box will prompt you to name the new separated region.

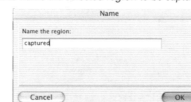

The new region shows the name given by you in the previous step.

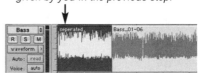

Heal Separation →

Command + H
PC: Ctrl + H

Select the regions you want to heal.

When you apply this shortcut the regions will become one. In other words, the vertical lines will disappear.

Command + L
PC: Ctrl + L

←Lock/Unlock Selected Region

When a region is locked, a small padlock will appear in the lower left corner of the region.

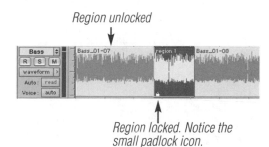

Region unlocked

Region locked. Notice the small padlock icon.

Type the first letter of the region you wish to select
(Enable the a–z box at top-right corner of the Audio Regions List)

PC: Type the first letter of the region you wish to select
(Enable the a–z box at top-right corner of the Audio Regions List)

Browse Regions
by Name (on Audio
Region List)

"Key Command Focus" must be enabled.

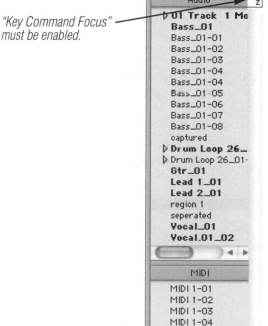

Shift + Command + B
PC: Shift + Ctrl + B

←Clear Selected Region(s)
from Audio Regions List

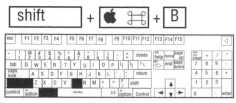

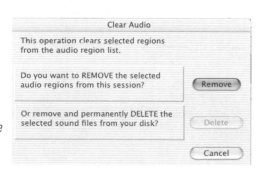

Be cautious with this dialog box! If you choose to "Remove" the selected regions, they will be removed from the session only. If you choose to "Delete" them, you will lose them forever. They will be erased from the hard disk.

Auditioning a Region in the Audio Regions List →

Option + Click & hold mouse button on region in Audio Regions List.

PC: Alt + Click & hold mouse button on region in Audio Regions List.

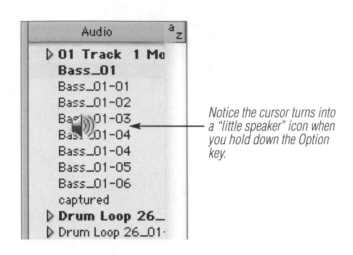

Option

Notice the cursor turns into a "little speaker" icon when you hold down the Option key.

Rename Region/File →

Double-Click region in the Audio Regions List or Double-Click with the Grabber tool on the region in the Playlist

PC: Double-Click region in Audio Regions List or Double-Click with Grabber on the region in the Playlist

Select the region and double-click with the Grabber tool.

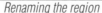

Renaming the region

The new region receives the name given by you in the previous step.

Constrain Region Placement to Start at Play/Edit Cursor Location or Selection Start →

Control + Click on region with Grabber Tool
(Not available in Shuffle and Spot modes)

**PC: Right Mouse Click on region with Grabber Tool
(Not available in Shuffle and Spot modes)**

Control + Click on selected region with Grabber tool

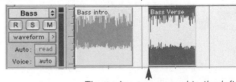

Place the cursor on the Timeline location where you want the region to begin.

When the shortcut is applied, the start point of the region will move to the cursor position.

Cursor

The region was moved to the left.

Command + ","
PC: Ctrl + ","

Set the edit cursor anywhere in the region and apply the shortcut.

NOTE: A "small triangle" icon appears pointing down.

◄—**Identify Sync Point**

Sync Point—

Command + I
PC: Ctrl + I

The conductor icon in the Transport window must be enabled for this command to take effect.

◄—**Identify Beat**

Command + A

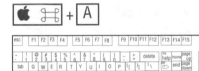

◄— **Select All**

Click the Tab key
PC: Click the Tab key

◄— **Go to Next Region Boundary/Sync Point**

Region Boundary

Pressing the Tab key will move the cursor to the next region boundary, no matter where your cursor is.

NOTE: The "Tab to Transient" button should be off (disabled); otherwise when you press the Tab key, the cursor will move to the next transient.

Next Region Boundary

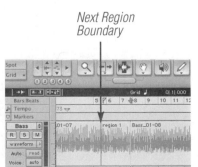

Go to Previous Region Boundary/Sync Point →

Option + Tab
PC: Ctrl + Tab

NOTE: The "Tab to Transient" button should be off (disabled); otherwise when you press the Tab key, the cursor will only move to the next transient.

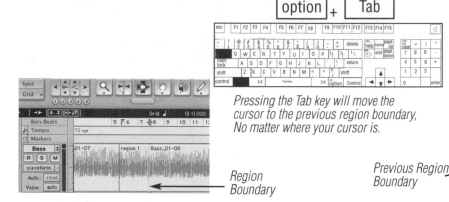

Pressing the Tab key will move the cursor to the previous region boundary, No matter where your cursor is.

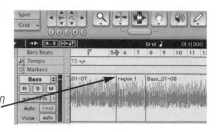

Region Boundary

Previous Region Boundary

Go to & Select Next Region →

Control + Tab
PC: Start + Tab

There is no need to make a selection, the shortcut will make the selection.

Go to & Select Previous Region →

Control + Option + Tab
PC: Start + Ctrl + Tab

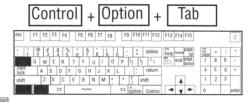

There is no need to make a selection; the shortcut will make the selection.

Shift + Tab
PC: Shift + Tab

← **Extend Selection to Next Region Boundary/Sync Point**

| Shift | + | Tab |

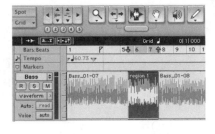

There is no need to have a selection already made. It will start making a selection from where your cursor is at the moment.

NOTE: The "Tab to Transient" button should be off (disabled); otherwise when you press the Tab key, the cursor will only move to the next transient.

Shift + Option + Tab
PC: Ctrl + Shift + Tab

← **Extend Selection to Previous Region Boundary/Sync Point**

| Shift | + | Option | + | Tab |

There is no need to have a selection already made. It will start making a selection from where your cursor is at the moment.

NOTE: The "Tab to Transient" button should be off (disabled); otherwise when you press the Tab key, the cursor will move to the next transient.

Shift + Control + Tab
PC: Start + Shift +Tab

← **Extend Selection to Include Next Region**

| Shift | + | Control | + | Tab |

There is no need to have a selection already made. It will start making a selection from where your cursor is at the moment.

NOTE: The "Tab to Transient" button should be off (disabled); otherwise when you press the Tab key, the cursor will move to the next transient.

35

Extend Selection to Include Previous Region → Shift + Control + Option + Tab
PC: Start + Shift + Ctrl + Tab

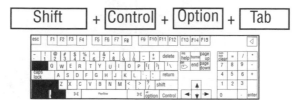

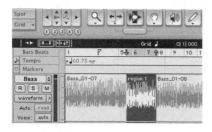

There is no need to have a selection already made. It will start making a selection from where your cursor is at the moment.

NOTE: The "Tab to Transient" button should be off (disabled); otherwise when you press the Tab key, the cursor will move to the next transient.

Extend Selection to Start of Session → Shift + Return
PC: Shift + Enter

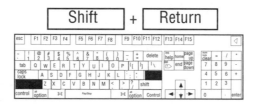

There is no need to have a selection already made. It will start making a selection from where your cursor is at the moment.

Extend Selection to End of Session → Shift + Option + Return
PC: Ctrl + Shift + Enter

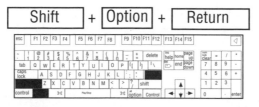

There is no need to have a selection already made. It will start making a selection from where your cursor is at the moment.

Down Arrow
PC: Down Arrow

← **<u>Set Selection Start during Playback</u>**

Notice the "blue arrows" in the Timeline are reset when you press the "down arrow." Next time you press Play, the new start time will be the one you selected when you pressed the "down arrow" during playback.

Up Arrow
PC: Up Arrow

← **<u>Set Selection End during Playback</u>**

Notice the "up arrow" in the Timeline changes position as you press the "up arrow" key during playback.

Double-Click quickly with Selector Tool
PC: Double-Click quickly with Selector Tool

← **<u>Select an Entire Region in a track in the Edit window</u>**

The "blue arrows" in the Timeline will change accordingly.

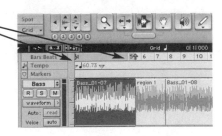

Command + "A" or Triple-Click quickly with Selector Tool
PC: Ctrl + A or Triple-Click quickly with Selector Tool

← **<u>Select All Regions in a Track in the Edit window</u>**

The "blue arrows" in the Timeline will change accordingly.

 +

Extend Selection to a Memory Location →

Shift + Period Key + Mem Loc Number (Numeric *) + Period key
PC: Shift + Period key + Mem Loc Number (Numeric *) + Period key

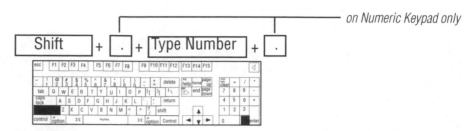

on Numeric Keypad only

Shift + . + Type Number + .

Memory Location

The selection was extended to the Memory Location.

Place Play/Edit Cursor or Create Selection across all Tracks →

Click and drag the Cursor with the Selector Tool in any timebase ruler

PC: Click and drag the Cursor with the Selector Tool in any timebase ruler

Timebase Rulers

NOTE: You must place the cursor on a "Timebase" ruler (Bars:Beats; Minutes:Seconds; TimeCode (TDM Systems only); Feet:Frames (TDM Systems only); Samples.

Extend Play/Edit Cursor or Selection across all Tracks →

Enable the "All" Edit Group (! Key) and Shift + Click on any other Track (or make selection in rulers)

PC: Enable "All" Edit Group (! key) and Shift + Click on any other Track

"blue arrows"

To Extend it:
- You must have a selection made first.
- Enable the "All" Group on the "Edit Groups" section.
- Click and hold the Shift key.
- While still pressing the Shift key, drag (extend) the selection to the desired side and length.
- Or click and drag any of the "blue arrows" to extend the selection. You don't need to hold down the Shift key.

The "All" Group in the Edit Groups Section

Shift + Click on each Track
PC: Shift + Click on each Track

← **Extend Play/Edit Cursor or Selection across more than one Track**

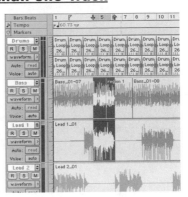

The cursor must be positioned first (using the Selector tool) within the area selected; then click the mouse to select the other Tracks.

Control + Option + "+/-" (Numeric *)
PC: Start + Alt + "+/-" (Numeric *)

← **Change Grid Value**

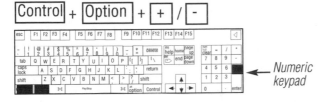

← Numeric keypad

Grid window

Option + Command + "+/-" (Numeric *)
PC: Ctrl + Alt + "+/-" (Numeric *)

← **Change Nudge Value**

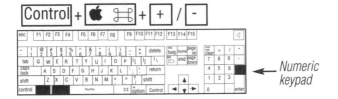

← Numeric keypad

Nudge window

"+/-" (Numeric *)
PC: "+/-" (Numeric *)

← **Nudge Selection or Region Right/Left by Nudge Value**

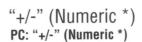

Numeric keypad

In this case, the region was nudged (moved) to the right. →

Nudge Data within current Region → to Left/Right by Nudge Value

Control + "+/-" (Numeric *)
PC: Start + "+/-" (Numeric *)

(Keeps region start/end and moves underlying audio)

← *Numeric keypad*

To do this:
- *Select a region.*
- *Hold down the Control key and start pressing the "-" or "+" on the numeric keypad.*
- *Notice the region will appear to go under the next region (-) or come out of it (+).*
- *You must set your Nudging interval.*

The waveforms look like they are going under the beginning of the track when you press the "+" key.

Nudge Left Selection Boundary Right/Left by Nudge Value →

Shift + Option + "+/-" (Numeric *)
PC: Alt + Shift + "+/-" (Numeric *)

The left side of the selection moved to the right after pressing Shift + Option and the "+" key once.

↖ *Start of selection (left)*

Nudge Right Selection Boundary → Right/Left by Nudge Value

Shift + Command + "+/-" (Numeric Keypad).
PC: Ctrl + Shift + "+/-" (Numeric Keypad).

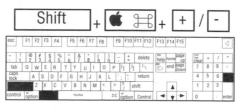

The right side of the selection moved to the right after pressing Shift + Command and the "+" key once.

↖ *End of selection (right)*

Option + "+/-" (Numeric *) → **Trim Left boundary of Region**
PC: Alt + Start + "+/-" (Numeric *) **to Right/Left by Nudge Value**

A selection must be made,
either by touching or going over
the boundary (edge) of a region,
for this shortcut to take effect.

Region's boundary   *Trimmed to the left*

Command + "+/-" (Numeric *) → **Trim Right boundary of Region**
PC: Ctrl + Start + "+/-" (Numeric *) **to Right/Left by Nudge Value**

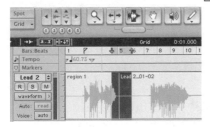

A selection must be made, by
either touching or going over
the boundary (edge) of a region,
for this shortcut to take effect.

Option + Trimmer Tool → **Reverse Trimmer Tool**
PC: Alt + Trimmer Tool **direction when trimming**
Region

Trimmer tool.   *Trimmer tool.*

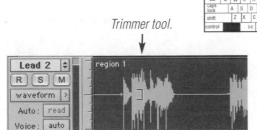

NOTE: You must select
the Trimmer tool first.

Notice the direction
of the Trimmer Tool
in each picture.

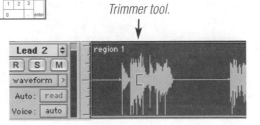

Trim Boundary between two Regions

→ Hold down the Command Key while Trimming
(only in Slip mode)

PC: Hold down the Ctrl Key while Trimming (only in Slip mode)

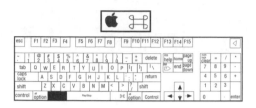

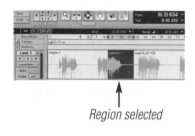

Region selected

Command + Trimming

Trimming

Notice the difference between the two actions: When "Command + Trimming," the region next to the one you are trimming will follow the trimming, while just trimming without holding the Command key will leave a space between the two regions.

Duplicate Region(s) in Edit window

→ Option + Click selection and drag to the desired destination

PC: Ctrl + Click selection and drag to the desired destination

Option + Click with Grabber tool

The Grabber tool must be selected first. You cannot accomplish this shortcut in Spot mode.

Original region

Original region

Region duplicated

Delete
PC: Backspace

← **Delete Selection in Edit window Playlist**

Delete

NOTE: This shortcut will remove the selected region from the track, but the original region will remain in the Audio Regions List.

To do this:
- Click the region with the Grabber tool once, or double-click on the region using the Selector tool.
- Then press the Delete Key.

Region selected to be deleted.

Region deleted from the track

Control + Move Audio Region with Grabber Tool
PC: Right Mouse Click and move Audio Region with Grabber Tool

← **Constrain Audio Region to vertical movement**

(This means that the region will not move horizontally.)

Control

- This does not apply if in Spot mode.
- MIDI region can also be moved vertically.
- You can only move a region vertically if both tracks are the same format, i.e., if both are mono or stereo. If you have a stereo track going into two mono tracks, this works as well.

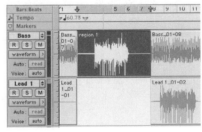

Control + Click Region with the Grabber Tool
PC: Start + Click Region with the Grabber Tool

← **Snap Region Start to Stationary Playhead or Edit Selection Start**

Control

Region start point
Cursor

This means that the Region start point will snap to wherever the cursor is located.

To do this:
- Set the cursor to the location you desire by simply clicking on a track.
- With the Grabber tool while holding down the Control key, click on the Region you need to move to the location the cursor is in.

Region start point
Cursor

43

Snap Region Start to Stationary Playhead or Edit Selection Sync Point →

Control + Option + Click new Region with Grabber
PC: Alt + Start + Click new Region with Grabber

Cursor

Duplicated region start point

NOTE: Does not work in Shuffle mode.

This shortcut will duplicate the region and will snap the start point of the duplicated region to where the cursor was located at the time of clicking on the region with the Grabber tool.

Snap Region End to Stationary Playhead or Edit Selection Start

→ Control + Command + Click Region with the Grabber
PC: Ctrl + Start + Click Region with the Grabber

NOTE: Does not work in Shuffle mode.

This shortcut will duplicate the region and will snap the end point of the duplicated region to where the cursor was located at the time of clicking on the region with the Grabber tool.

Region to be duplicated and moved

Duplicated and moved region

Create Fades window →

Command + F
PC: Ctrl + F

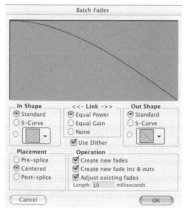

Fades window

NOTE: In order to apply this shortcut, there should be a selection made spanning two regions (crossfade), between the beginning of the track and the start point of a region (fade in), and between the end point of a region and the end of a track (fade out).

Control + Command + F (Uses default fade shape) ← **Apply Crossfade to**
PC: Ctrl + Start + F (uses last selected fade shape) **Selection without**
accessing Fades
window

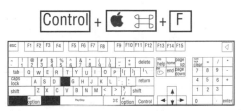

NOTE: Make sure there is a selection
made between two regions.

Option + Click + drag fade-in curve ← **Edit Fade-in only**
(In "None" Link mode only) **in Fades window**
PC: Alt + Click + drag fade-in curve (In "None" Link mode only) **(Crossfade only)**

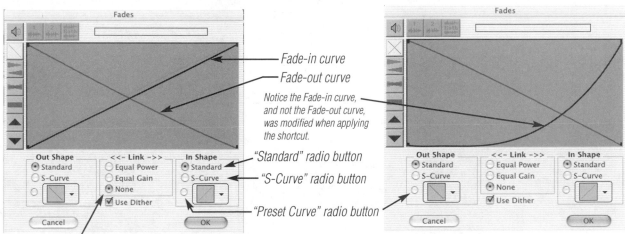

Fade-in curve
Fade-out curve

Notice the Fade-in curve,
and not the Fade-out curve,
was modified when applying
the shortcut.

"Standard" radio button
"S-Curve" radio button
"Preset Curve" radio button

"None" Link mode

NOTE: The "Standard" or "S-Curve" buttons must be chosen.
This does not work with "Preset Curve" button selected.

Once you have the "Fades" window on the screen, click
and drag the red curve (In Shape), while holding down
the Option Key. You will notice only the red curve will
move and not the blue one (Out Shape). Remember that
you must assign the Link mode to "None."

Edit Fade-out only in Fades window (Crossfade only) →

Command + Click + drag fade-out curve
(In "None" Link mode only)
PC: Ctrl + Click + drag fade-out curve (in "None" Link mode only)

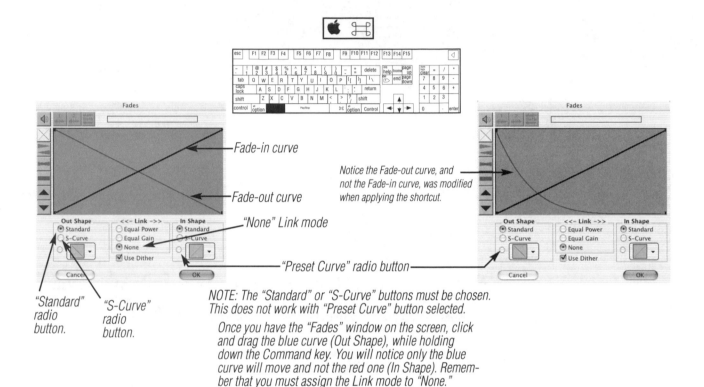

Fade-in curve

Fade-out curve

Notice the Fade-out curve, and not the Fade-in curve, was modified when applying the shortcut.

"None" Link mode

"Preset Curve" radio button

"Standard" radio button.

"S-Curve" radio button.

NOTE: The "Standard" or "S-Curve" buttons must be chosen. This does not work with "Preset Curve" button selected.

Once you have the "Fades" window on the screen, click and drag the blue curve (Out Shape), while holding down the Command key. You will notice only the blue curve will move and not the red one (In Shape). Remember that you must assign the Link mode to "None."

Audition Start/Stop in Fades window →

Spacebar
PC: Spacebar

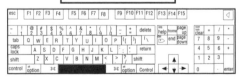

"Small speaker" icon

Pressing the Spacebar is the same as pressing the "small speaker" icon. When audition starts, the "small speaker" icon will be highlighted until you press the Spacebar again.

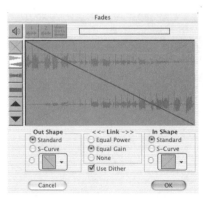

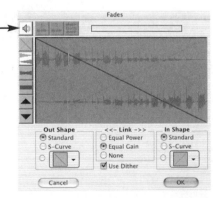

Command + Click on either zoom arrow
PC: Ctrl + Click on either zoom arrow

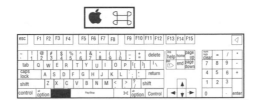

Reset to Default Zoom in Fades window

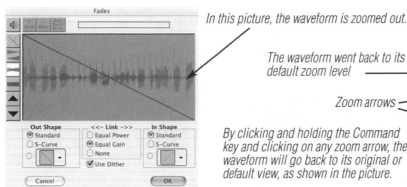

In this picture, the waveform is zoomed out.

The waveform went back to its default zoom level

Zoom arrows

By clicking and holding the Command key and clicking on any zoom arrow, the waveform will go back to its original or default view, as shown in the picture.

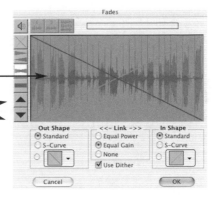

Control + Up/Down arrows
PC: Start + Up/Down arrows

Cycle up/down through Out Shape Parameter Options
In Fades window

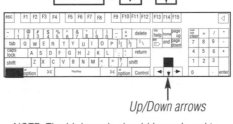

"None" Link mode button.

Up/Down arrows

NOTE: The Link mode should be assigned to "None." If not, both the Out Shape and the In Shape will move together.

Out Shape Parameter Options

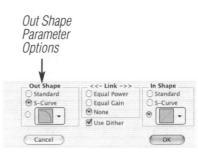

Option + Up/Down arrows
PC: Alt + Up/Down arrows

Cycle Up/Down through In Shape Parameter Options
In Fades window

"None" Link mode button.

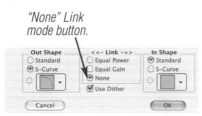

Up/Down arrows

NOTE: The Link mode should be assigned to "None." If not, both the Out Shape and the In Shape will move together.

In Shape Parameter Options

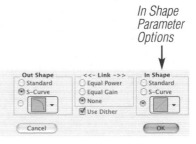

Cycle Up/Down through Link Parameter Options

In Fades window

→ Up/Down arrows
PC: Up/Down arrows

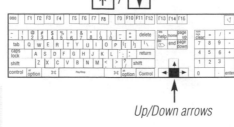

Link Parameter Options

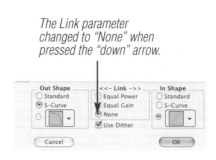

Up/Down arrows

The Link parameter changed to "None" when pressed the "down" arrow.

Cycle Up/Down through Preset Out Shape curves

In Fades window

→ Control + Left/Right arrows
PC: Start + Left/Right arrows

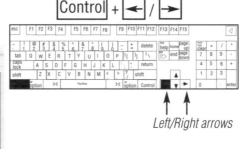

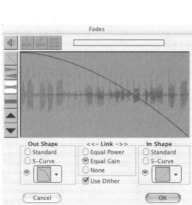

Left/Right arrows

NOTE: The Link parameter should be assigned to "None." If not, both the Out and In Shape Curves will change simultaneously.

Out Shape Curves →

Cycle Up/Down through Preset In Shape curves

In Fades window

→ Option + Left/Right arrows
PC: Alt + Left/Right arrows

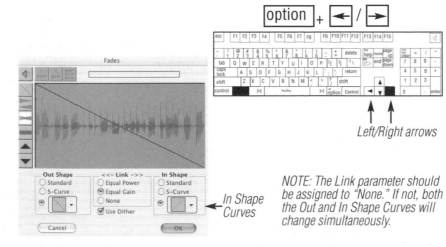

Left/Right arrows

In Shape Curves

NOTE: The Link parameter should be assigned to "None." If not, both the Out and In Shape Curves will change simultaneously.

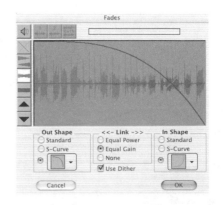

Enter Key (Numeric Keypad) ← **Create a Memory Location**
PC: Enter (Numeric Keypad)

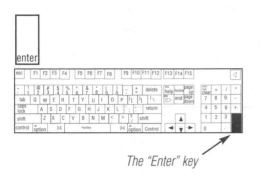

The "Enter" key

NOTE: When creating a Memory Location while in Playback mode, you can enable the "Auto-name Memory Locations when playing" option located in Setups > Preferences > Editing. With this option enabled, Pro Tools won't ask you to name the "Marker" when you create one while playing back the Session. You can create up to 200 Memory Locations in Pro Tools.

Control + Click on Memory Location ← **Reset a Memory Location**
PC: Start + Click on Memory Location Button

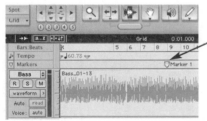

Memory Location

NOTE: You can reset a Memory Location to change its name, zoom settings, etc. Also, you can just double-click on the Memory Location to change its properties.

Option + Click on a Memory Location ← **Delete a Memory Location**
PC: Alt + Click on a Memory Location button

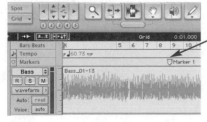

Memory Location

Same place, memory location was deleted.

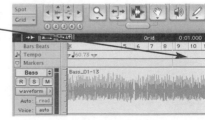

To delete a Memory Location from the Edit window, you can also click and drag down the "Marker" from the Marker Ruler. You will notice a small "Trash can" icon appearing when dragging the marker down.

Recall a Memory Location →

Period key + Memory Location
Number (Numeric *) + Period key

**PC: Period key + Mem. Location Number (Numeric *)
+ Period key or Click on Mem. Location Button**

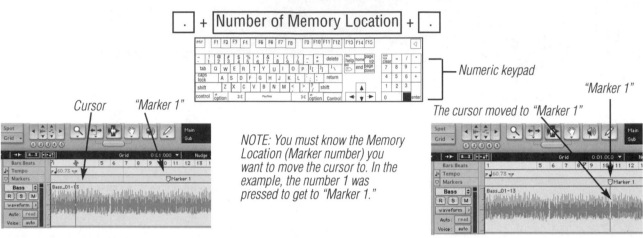

. + Number of Memory Location + .

Numeric keypad

Cursor   *"Marker 1"*   *"Marker 1"*

The cursor moved to "Marker 1"

NOTE: You must know the Memory
Location (Marker number) you
want to move the cursor to. In the
example, the number 1 was
pressed to get to "Marker 1."

Temporary Scrub mode when Using Selector →

Control + Click and drag

**PC: Right mouse Click and
drag or Start + Click and drag**

Selector tool

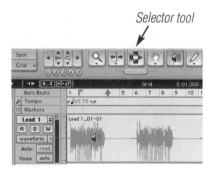

NOTE: You must have the
Selector tool enabled.

Control

Extend Selection while Scrubbing →

Shift + Click and drag with Scrubber (also in Temporary Scrub mode)

PC: Shift + Click and drag with Scrubber (also in Temporary Scrub mode)

Scrubber tool

NOTE: You must have the Scrubber
tool enabled. You can also accomplish
this with the Selector tool by holding
down the Control and Shift keys.

Shift

MIX & EDIT GROUPS

Grouping affects: Volume level/faders, solos and mutes, automation modes, track display format, track height, editing and playlist enables.

Does not affect: Record enables, pan, voice and output assignments, and creating instances of TDM Plug-Ins.

Command + G
PC: Ctrl + G

← **Group Selected Tracks**

NOTE: You must first select the name of the tracks you desire to group. Also, you can select the Group ID as desired, up to 26 ID letters.

Control + Any operation that affects Groups
PC: Start + Left Mouse Click-any operation that affects groups or Right Click-any operation that affects Groups

← **Temporarily Isolate Channel Strip from Group Operation**

This will temporarily disable the Group Edits.

This is used to change the parameters of one track without affecting the entire group. Notice the track size change on track "Audio 2" and not on all the tracks in the group.

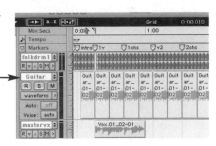

Shift + Command + G
or Command + Click on Edit Groups menu
PC: Ctrl + Shift + G or Ctrl + Click on Edit Groups menu

← **Suspend/Resume All Groups**

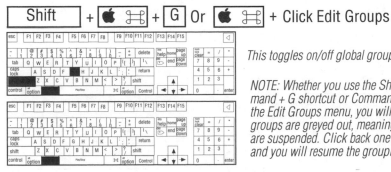

This toggles on/off global group edits.

NOTE: Whether you use the Shift + Command + G shortcut or Command + Click on the Edit Groups menu, you will notice all groups are greyed out, meaning the groups are suspended. Click back one more time, and you will resume the groupings.

Edit Groups menu

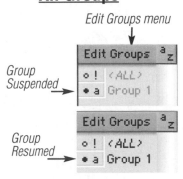

Group Suspended

Group Resumed

Rename Group → Double-Click to far left of group name in the Edit Groups List
PC: Double-Click to far left of group name in the Edit Groups List

NOTE: Make sure you click right on the left of the Group you want to rename.

Group Enable/Disable → Type ID letter on keyboard
(To enable keyboard selection of Groups, click a-z box at top right of Edit Groups List)
PC: Type ID letter on keyboard
(To enable keyboard selection of Groups, click a-z box at top right of Edit Groups List)

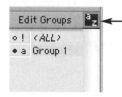 ← *a–z box (this will turn off the a–z box below the Zoom buttons in the Edit window)*

When you enable or disable a Group by typing the letter of the Group ID, you will notice that the Group name selected will be highlighted (enabled) or dehighlighted (disabled) when applying this shortcut.

Show Group Members only → Control + Click on group in Edit Groups List
PC: Right Mouse Click on group(s) in Edit Groups List or Shift + Click

Control + click on Edit Groups

All Groups and tracks showing

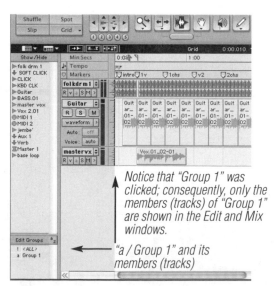

Notice that "Group 1" was clicked; consequently, only the members (tracks) of "Group 1" are shown in the Edit and Mix windows.

"a / Group 1" and its members (tracks)

Shift + Control + Click in Edit Groups List → **Show Group Members only (For multiple Groups)**
PC: Shift + Start + Left Mouse Click or Shift + Right Mouse Click

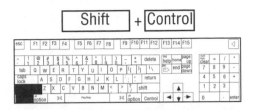

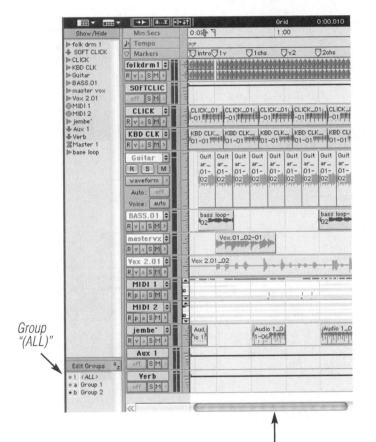

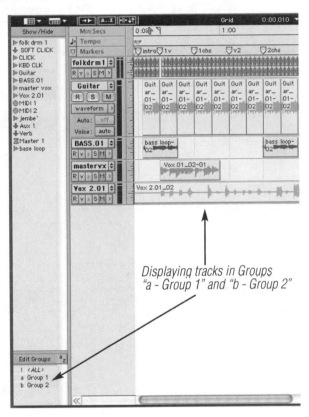

Displaying tracks in Groups "a - Group 1" and "b - Group 2"

Group "(ALL)"

Displaying all the tracks from the "(ALL)" Group

NOTE: You must first press Control and click on the Group you want to show, then add the Shift key to keep selecting other Groups to be shown. Otherwise, if you don't, the Group you want to show will be hidden instead. A good way to hide specific Groups is by holding down Control + Shift and clicking on the Group you want to hide.

MIDI

Quantize →

Option + Ø (on Alphanumeric or Numeric Keypad)
PC: Alt + Ø (on Alphanumeric or Numeric Keypad)

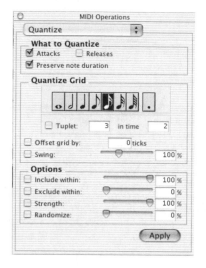

NOTE: You must make a selection of some MIDI notes to apply the "Quantize" command.

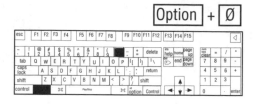

NOTE: You can hold down the Command key + up/down arrows (PC: Ctrl = up/down arrows) to cycle through the "MIDI Operations" functions.

Transpose →

Option + T
PC: Alt + T

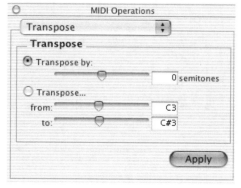

NOTE: You must make a selection of some MIDI notes to apply the "Transpose" command.

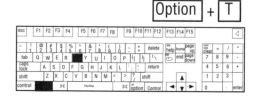

NOTE: You can hold down the Command key + up/down arrows (PC: Ctrl = up/down arrows) to cycle through the "MIDI Operations" functions.

Select Notes →

Option + P
PC: Alt + P

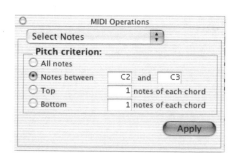

NOTE: You must make a selection of some MIDI notes to apply the "Select Notes" command.

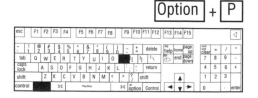

NOTE: You can hold down the Command key + up/down arrows (PC: Ctrl = up/down arrows) to cycle through the "MIDI Operations" functions.

Option + Y
PC: Alt + Y

← **Split Notes**

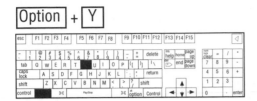

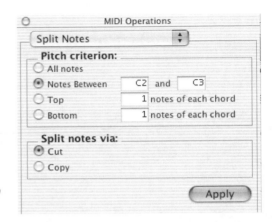

NOTE: You must make a selection of some MIDI notes to apply the "Split Notes" command.

NOTE: You can hold down the Command key + up/down arrows (PC: Ctrl = up/down arrows) to cycle through the "MIDI Operations" functions.

Shift + Command + "." (Period Key)
PC: Ctrl + Shift + "."

← **All Notes Off**

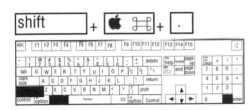

NOTE: This shortcut will send an "All Notes Off" MIDI command to each channel for all the MIDI devices in your studio, in the event that you encounter "stuck notes" (sounds that are "on" without being able to turn them off in a conventional manner with any of your MIDI devices). The "All Notes Off" MIDI command will turn those sounds (stuck notes) off.

MIDI EVENT LIST ENTRY

*The following commands are active only
when the MIDI Event List Window is open.*

Enter Start Time field for Editing → Command + Enter (Numeric Keypad)
PC: Ctrl + Enter (Numeric Keypad)

*This shortcut will select the first "Start Time" field
for editing. After this, you can cycle through the
other fields to the right, if desired, using the
up/down arrows and releasing the Command key.*

Show Event Filter dialog → Command + F
PC: Ctrl + F

*This dialog window allows you
to specify which MIDI event
types are displayed in the MIDI
Event List.*

Command + G
PC: Ctrl + G

← **Go to**

This dialog window will allow you to position the cursor to the specified location. Notice the cursor will go to the location prior the desired one when you apply the "Go to" command.

Command + H
PC: Ctrl + H

← **Scroll to Edit Selection**

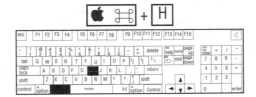

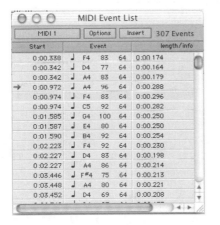

You can also do this by simply using the up/down arrows.

Command + M
PC: Ctrl + M

← **Insert Another Event**

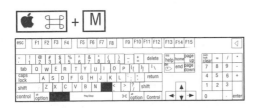

This allows you to insert another MIDI event of the same type as the one you inserted earlier.

Insert Note →

Command + N
PC: Ctrl + N

Icon indicating "Note"

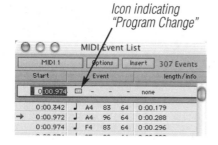

This allows you to insert a MIDI note in the MIDI Event List.

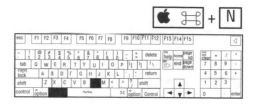

Insert Program Change →

Command + P
PC: Ctrl + P

Icon indicating "Program Change"

This allows you to insert a "Program Change" command. In other words, a different sound or preset from your synthesizer or other MIDI sound modules (samplers, drum machines, etc.).

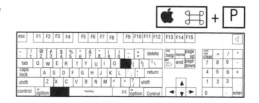

Insert Controller →

Command + L
PC: Ctrl + L

Icon indicating "Controller"

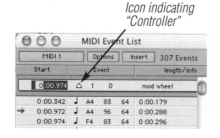

This allows you to insert a different MIDI Controller.

Insert Poly Pressure →

Command + O
PC: Ctrl + O

Icon indicating "Poly Pressure"

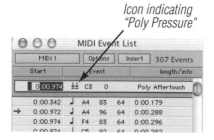

This allows you to insert a "Poly Pressure" MIDI command.

Option + Click on Event
PC: Alt + Click on Event

←Delete Event in MIDI Event List

Option

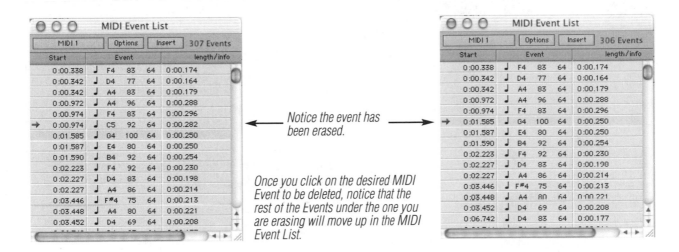

MIDI Event List			
MIDI 1	Options	Insert	307 Events
Start	Event		length/info
0:00.338	♩ F4 83 64		0:00.174
0:00.342	♩ D4 77 64		0:00.164
0:00.342	♩ A4 83 64		0:00.179
0:00.972	♩ A4 96 64		0:00.288
0:00.974	♩ F4 83 64		0:00.296
→ 0:00.974	♩ C5 92 64		0:00.282
0:01.585	♩ G4 100 64		0:00.250
0:01.587	♩ E4 80 64		0:00.250
0:01.590	♩ B4 92 64		0:00.254
0:02.223	♩ F4 92 64		0:00.230
0:02.227	♩ D4 83 64		0:00.198
0:02.227	♩ A4 86 64		0:00.214
0:03.446	♩ F#4 75 64		0:00.213
0:03.448	♩ A4 80 64		0:00.221
0:03.452	♩ D4 69 64		0:00.208

← Notice the event has been erased. →

Once you click on the desired MIDI Event to be deleted, notice that the rest of the Events under the one you are erasing will move up in the MIDI Event List.

MIDI Event List			
MIDI 1	Options	Insert	306 Events
Start	Event		length/info
0:00.338	♩ F4 83 64		0:00.174
0:00.342	♩ D4 77 64		0:00.164
0:00.342	♩ A4 83 64		0:00.179
0:00.972	♩ A4 96 64		0:00.288
0:00.974	♩ F4 83 64		0:00.296
→ 0:01.585	♩ G4 100 64		0:00.250
0:01.587	♩ E4 80 64		0:00.250
0:01.590	♩ B4 92 64		0:00.254
0:02.223	♩ F4 92 64		0:00.230
0:02.227	♩ D4 83 64		0:00.198
0:02.227	♩ A4 86 64		0:00.214
0:03.446	♩ F#4 75 64		0:00.213
0:03.448	♩ A4 80 64		0:00.221
0:03.452	♩ D4 69 64		0:00.208
0:06.742	♩ D4 83 64		0:00.177

NUMERIC ENTRY OPTIONS

**<u>Initiate Time Entry
in Current Location
& Big Counter</u>** → **"=" or "*" on Numeric Keypad**

PC: * on Numeric Keypad

This works on the "Main" counter, "Transport window" counter, and "Big Counter." The "Big Counter" window or the "Transport window" has to be shown for this to apply.

0 : 01.585

**<u>Initiate Time Entry
in Edit window
Start/End/Length fields</u>** → **"/" (Numeric Keypad)** (Subsequent presses toggle through fields)

PC: / (Numeric Keypad) (Subsequent presses toggle through fields)

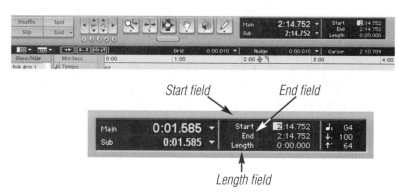

Start field   *End field*

Length field

**<u>Initiate Time Entry
in Transport
window field</u>** → **Option + "/" (Numeric Keypad)** (Subsequent presses toggle through fields)

PC: Alt + / (Numeric Keypad) (Subsequent presses toggle through fields)

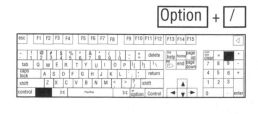

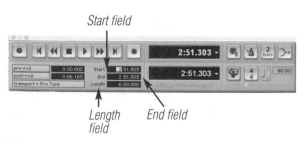

Start field

Length field   *End field*

"=" (hold key down for continued input)
PC: = (hold key down for continued input)

← **<u>Capture Incoming Timecode in Session Setup window</u>** <u>(with Start field Selected)</u>, **<u>Spot dialog & Time Stamp Selected dialog</u>**

This must have incoming Timecode signal in order to function.

Session Start field selected

"." Period Key
PC: Period Key

← **<u>Move Sub-unit Selection to the right</u>**

You can also use the "." key from the Numeric Keypad. Notice if you keep pressing the "." key, you can cycle through all the fields from left to right.

Sub-unit selection

Sub-unit selection moved to the right

Left/Right arrows
PC: Left/Right arrows

← **<u>Move Sub-unit Selection to the left/right</u>**

Sub-unit selection moved to the left →

Sub-unit selection

"+" or "−" Keys followed by offset number ← **<u>"Calculator Entry" mode</u>**
PC: + or - Keys followed by offset number

Will add or substract the length given after pressing "Enter." It turns into a calculator.
In order to do this:
- Select a field you want to change.
- Press the "+" key (numeric keypad) for adding or the "-" key for subtracting.
- Type the number desired.
- Press the Enter key.

Increment/Decrement the current Sub-unit →

Up/Down arrows
PC: Up/Down arrows

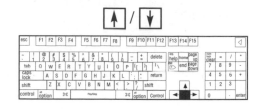

← *Sub-unit in start field decremented by pressing the "Down" arrow key two times.* →

Clear Entered Numeric Value & Stay in Time Entry mode →

Delete
PC: Backspace

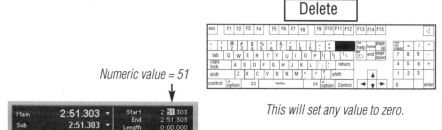

Numeric value = 51

This will set any value to zero.

Numeric value cleared to "Ø".

Apply Entered Numeric Value →

Return or Enter
PC: Enter

Numeric value entered

Numeric value applied

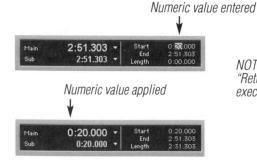

NOTE: You must always press the "Return" or the "Enter" keys to execute the numeric value change.

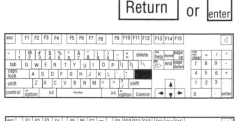

Esc
PC: Esc

← <u>**Clear Entered Numeric Value and Exit Time Entry mode**</u>

Numeric Value entered

Numeric Value cleared and Time Entry mode off

NOTE: After pressing the "Esc" key, the number you have typed will disappear and the number that was there before the change will be shown. If you press the "Delete" key, then the number will be set to zero. Remember to press the "Return" or "Enter" key to apply or execute.

MIX WINDOW
(All these commands take place in the Mix window)

<u>Set All Faders to their</u> <u>Automation Null Points</u> → Option + Clicking on either Automatch triangle
PC: Alt + Click on either Automatch triangle

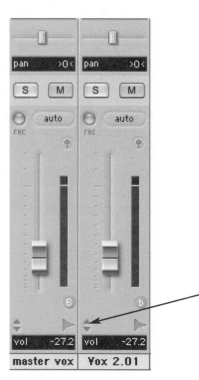

When you press the Option key and click on any Automatch triangle, the fader will return to the last recorded (automated) level. In other words, if you make a fader automation move, and then you move that fader, when you apply this shortcut the fader will return to the last recorded fader move or level.

Automatch triangle

<u>Reset a Control to</u> <u>Default Value</u> → Option + Click on control
PC: Alt + Click on control

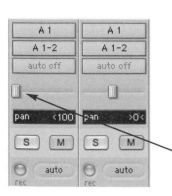

You can reset any volume fader, pan slider, etc., to its default position by pressing Option and clicking on the fader or pan slider. For panning, this will return the slider to the center position; for volume the fader will be set to 0 dB.

The pan slider is set to the left before applying the shortcut.

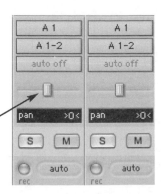

The pan slider was set back to the center position after applying the shortcut.

Click on Headroom Indicator
PC: Click on Headroom Indicator

← **<u>Clear Peak/clip-hold from Meter</u>**

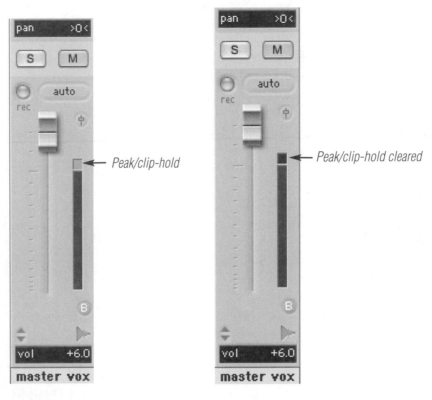

Peak/clip-hold

Peak/clip-hold cleared

Command + Click on Insert name in Inserts view   ← **<u>Bypass Plug-In Insert</u>**
PC: Ctrl + Click on Insert name in Inserts view

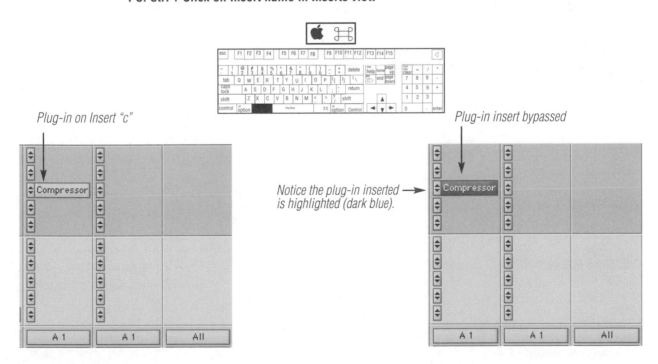

Plug-in on Insert "c"

*Notice the plug-in inserted →
is highlighted (dark blue).*

Plug-in insert bypassed

<u>Send Mute</u> → Command + Click on Send name in Sends view
PC: Ctrl + Click on Send name in Sends view

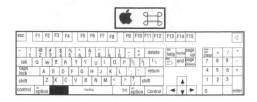

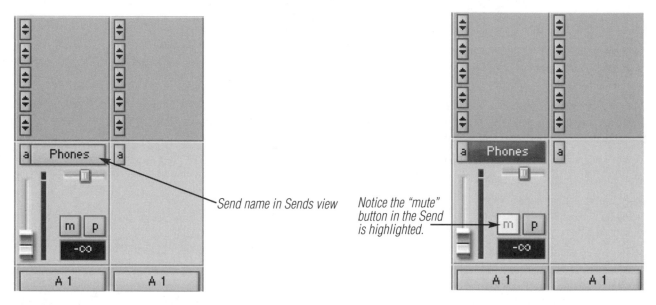

Send name in Sends view

Notice the "mute" button in the Send is highlighted.

<u>Toggle Send Display between "All" & "Individual" mode</u> → Command + Click on Send diamond
PC: Ctrl + Click on Send diamond

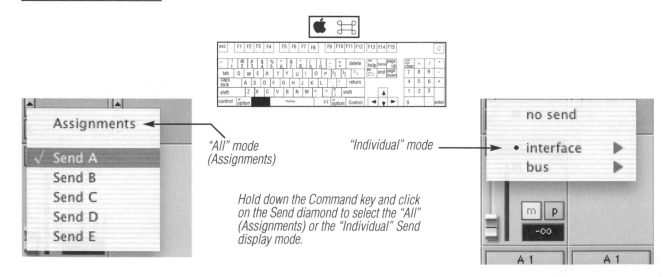

"All" mode (Assignments)

"Individual" mode

Hold down the Command key and click on the Send diamond to select the "All" (Assignments) or the "Individual" Send display mode.

IMPORT AUDIO DIALOG

Shift + Command + I
PC: Ctrl + Shift + I

← **<u>Show Import Audio window from the audio pop-up menu</u>**

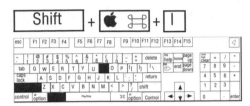

Import Audio window

Return or Enter
PC: Enter

← **<u>Add Currently Selected Region or Audio File to List</u>**

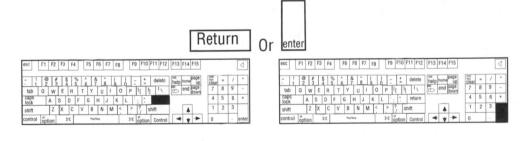

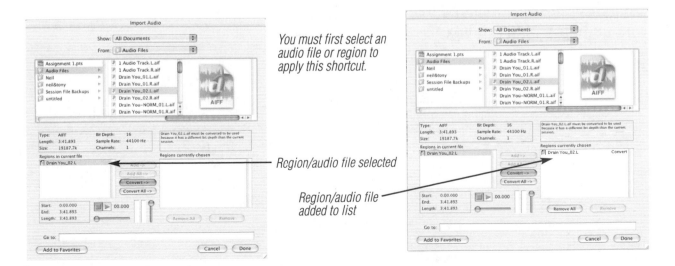

You must first select an audio file or region to apply this shortcut.

Region/audio file selected

Region/audio file added to list

<u>Audition Currently Selected Audio File or Region</u>

→ Command + P or Spacebar
PC: Spacebar

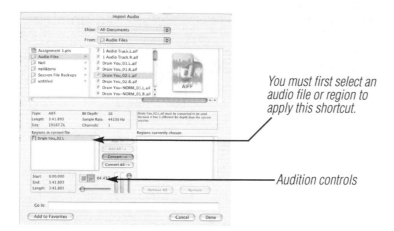

You must first select an audio file or region to apply this shortcut.

Audition controls

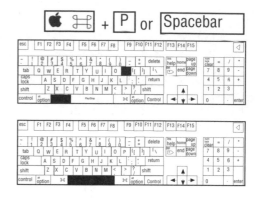

<u>Stop Audition of Selected File and Retain Selection</u>

→ Command + P or Command + S
PC: Spacebar

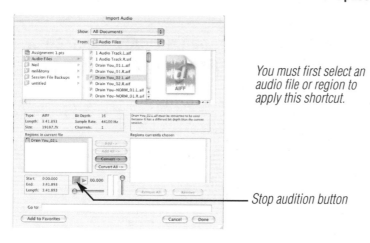

You must first select an audio file or region to apply this shortcut.

Stop audition button

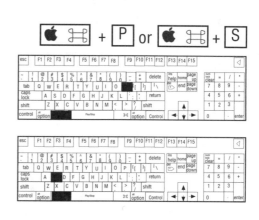

<u>Stop Audition of Selected File and go to top of scroll box</u>

→ Spacebar
PC: Home

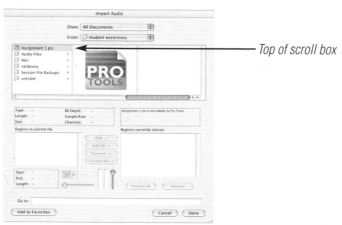

Top of scroll box

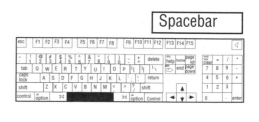

Tab   ← **Move between File windows**
PC: Tab

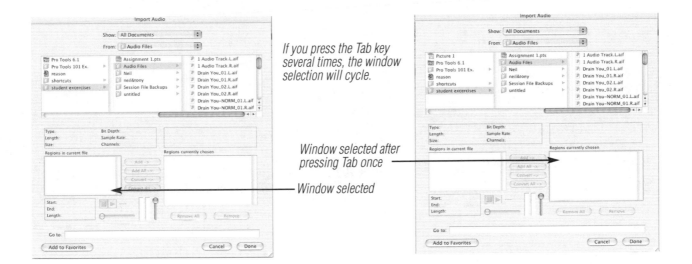

If you press the Tab key several times, the window selection will cycle.

Window selected after pressing Tab once

Window selected

Command + W   ← **Done**
PC: Alt + E

NOTE: By pressing the "Done" button, the "Import Audio" window will be closed.

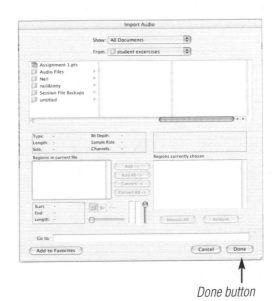

Done button

Cancel →

Command + "." Period Key (on alphanumeric or numeric keypad)
PC: Esc or Alt + C

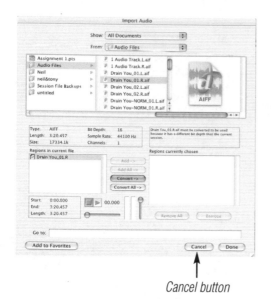

NOTE: By pressing "Cancel," the "Audio Import" window will be closed.

Cancel button

Random-Access Fwd/Rew Search through Selected File →

Click and move slider to the desired time location
PC: Drag slider to desired time location

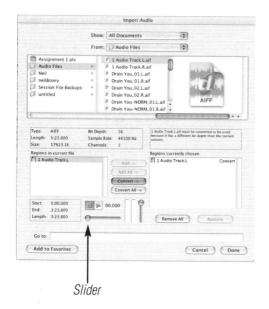

Slider

CONVERT AND IMPORT DIALOG

The following shortcuts are active only when the "Import Audio" dialog window is shown.

Command + C
PC: Alt + O

←**Convert**

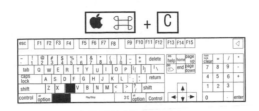

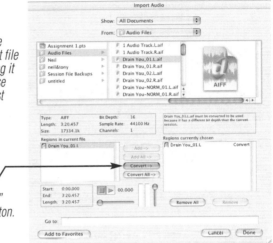
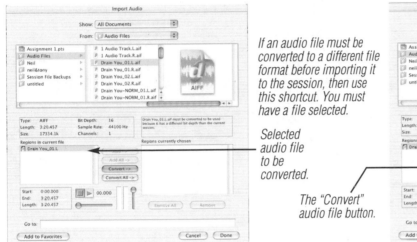

If an audio file must be converted to a different file format before importing it to the session, then use this shortcut. You must have a file selected.

Selected audio file to be converted.

The "Convert" audio file button.

Command + R
PC: Alt + R

←**Remove**

You must select the file you wish to remove from the Import list.

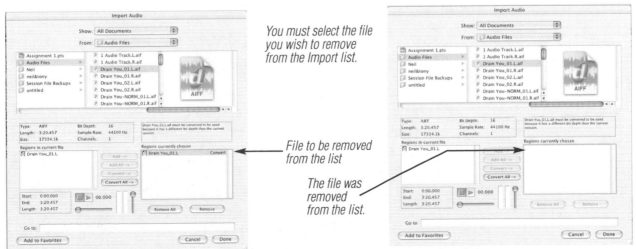

File to be removed from the list

The file was removed from the list.

Add All →

Command + Option + A
PC: Start + Alt + A

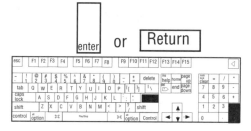

Selected files to be added

You must first select all the audio files you wish to add to the list.

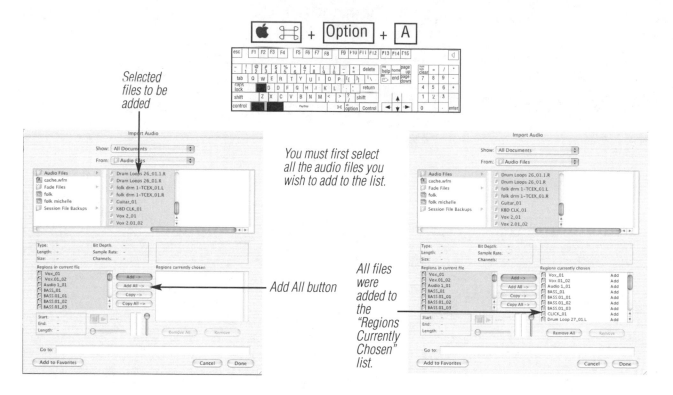

Add All button

All files were added to the "Regions Currently Chosen" list.

Import Current Selection →

Enter or Return
PC: Enter

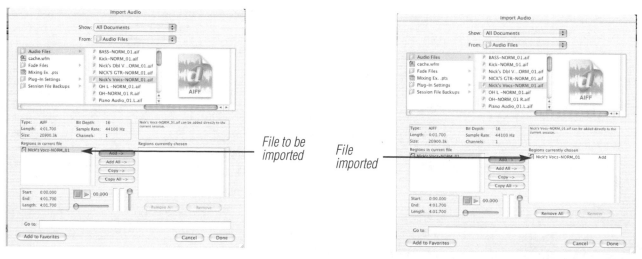

File to be imported

File imported

Shift + Command + I
PC: N/A
→ **Import All**

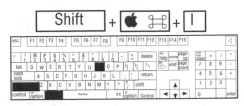

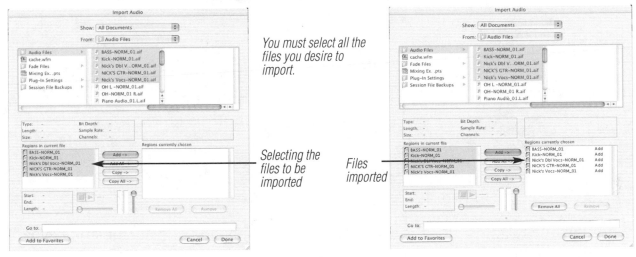

You must select all the files you desire to import.

Selecting the files to be imported

Files imported

Shift + Command + R
PC: Alt + R
← **Remove All Items from List**

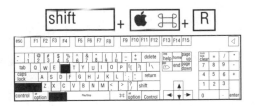

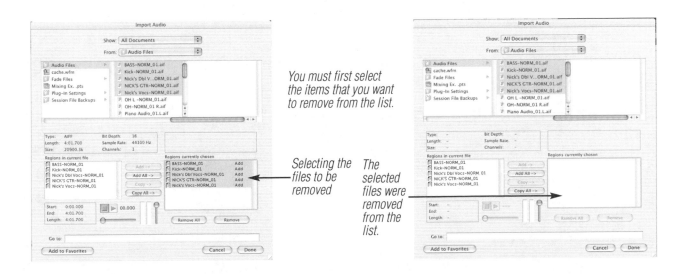

You must first select the items that you want to remove from the list.

Selecting the files to be removed

The selected files were removed from the list.

PERIPHERALS DIALOG

The following shortcuts are active only when the "Peripherals" dialog window is shown (Setups > Peripherals).

Go to Synchronization window →

Command + 1(on Alphanumeric or Numeric Keypad)
PC: Ctrl + 1

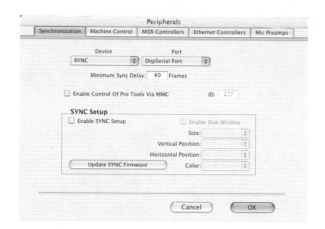

Use this window to make all your synchronizer's settings.

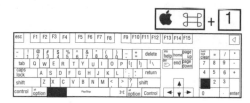

Go to Machine Control window →

Command + 2 (on Alphanumeric or Numeric Keypad)
PC: Ctrl + 2

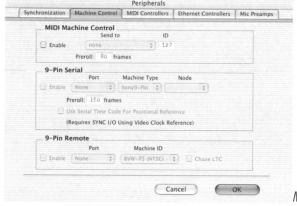

Use this window to make all your "Machine Control" settings.

Machine Control window

Go to MIDI Controllers window →

Command + 3 (on Alphanumeric or Numeric Keypad)
PC: Ctrl + 3

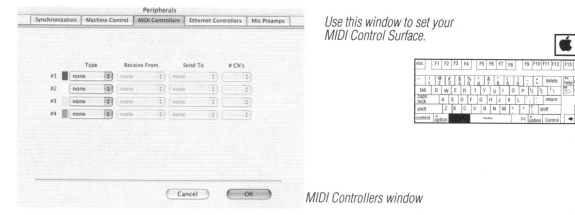

Use this window to set your MIDI Control Surface.

MIDI Controllers window

Command + 4 (on Alphanumeric or Numeric Keypad)
PC: Ctrl + 4
← **Go to Ethernet Controllers window**

Use this window to set your Ethernet control surface.

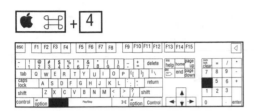

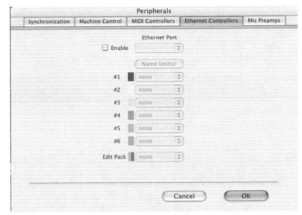

Ethernet Controllers window

Command + 5
PC: Ctrl + 5
← **Go to Mic Preamps window**

Use this window to set all your mic preamplifiers.

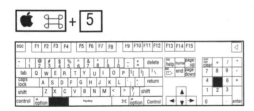

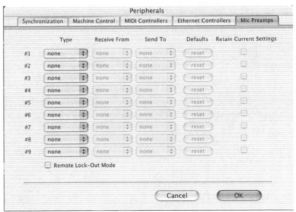

Mic Preamps window

PREFERENCES DIALOG

In order for these shortcuts to take effect, you must first select the "Preferences" dialog window (Setups > Preferences). The numbers can be accessed from the Alphanumeric or the Numeric Keypad.

Go to Display window →

Command + 1
PC: Ctrl + 1

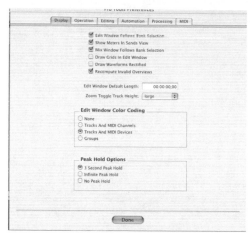

Display window

Go to Operation window →

Command + 2
PC: Ctrl + 2

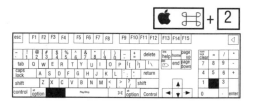

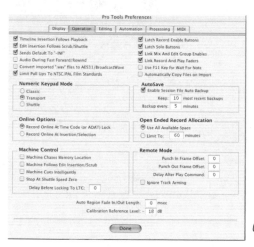

Operation window

Go to Editing window →

Command + 3
PC: Ctrl + 3

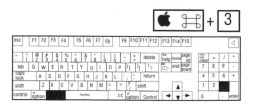

Editing window

Command + 4
PC: Ctrl + 4

← **Go to Automation window**

Automation window

Command + 5
PC: Ctrl + 5

← **Go to Processing window**

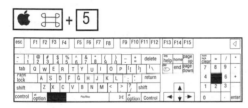

Processing window

<u>Go to MIDI window</u>→

Command + 6

PC: Ctrl + 6

MIDI window

PLUG-IN SETTINGS LIBRARIAN

Shift + Command + S
PC: Ctrl + Shift + S

← **Save Settings**

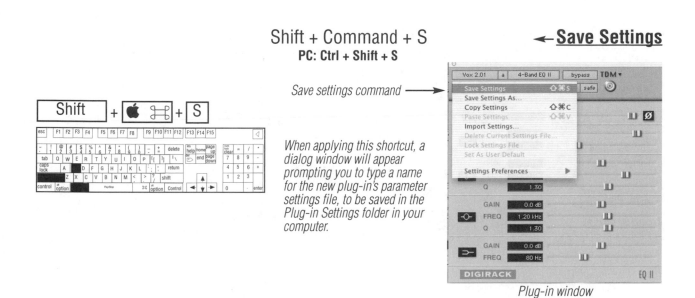

Save settings command ——→

When applying this shortcut, a dialog window will appear prompting you to type a name for the new plug-in's parameter settings file, to be saved in the Plug-in Settings folder in your computer.

Plug-in window

Shift + Command + C
PC: Ctrl + Shift + C

← **Copy Settings**

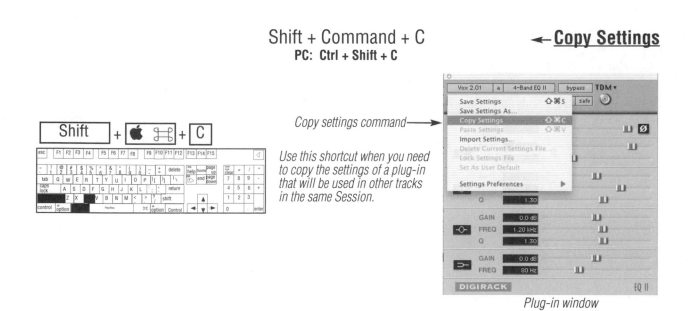

Copy settings command ——→

Use this shortcut when you need to copy the settings of a plug-in that will be used in other tracks in the same Session.

Plug-in window

Paste Settings→

Shift + Command + V

PC: Ctrl + Shift + V

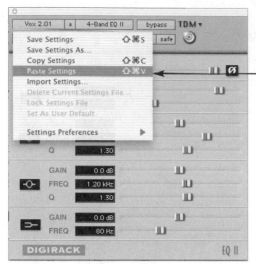

Plug-in window

Paste settings command

Use this shortcut to paste the plug-in settings you copied on another track, using the same plug-in in the same Session.

KEYBOARD INPUT FOR PLUG-IN PARAMETERS

Click mouse in text field
PC: Click mouse in text field

← **Type Desired Value**

Click in text field and type value. Use this to enter the desired values quickly instead of guessing the value by moving the parameter sliders on any plug-in.

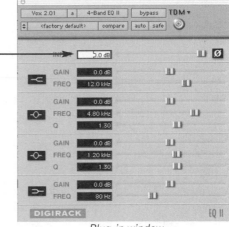

Plug-in window

Tab or Shift + Tab
PC: Tab or Shift + Tab

← **Move Down/Up Parameter field**

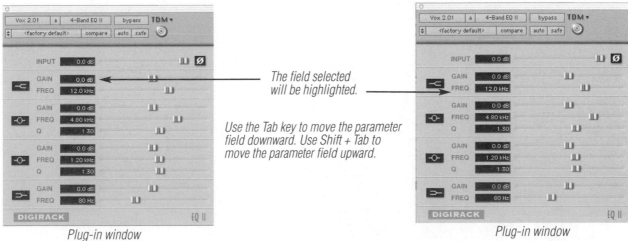

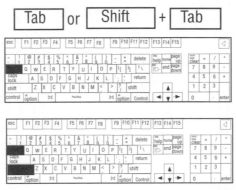

The field selected will be highlighted.

Use the Tab key to move the parameter field downward. Use Shift + Tab to move the parameter field upward.

Plug-in window

Plug-in window

Increase/Decrease Slider Value → Up/Down arrows
PC: Up/Down arrows

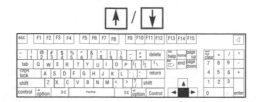

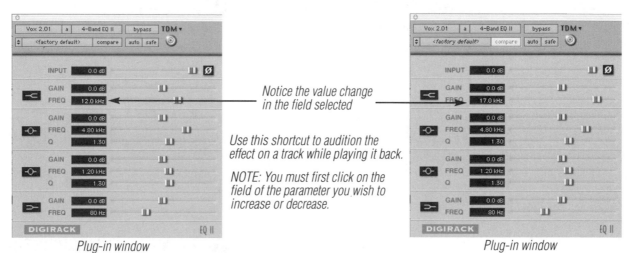

*Notice the value change
in the field selected*

*Use this shortcut to audition the
effect on a track while playing it back.*

*NOTE: You must first click on the
field of the parameter you wish to
increase or decrease.*

Plug-in window　　　　　*Plug-in window*

Input Value without leaving the field
Enter
PC: Enter (Numeric Keypad)

Selected field

*Selected field with the
new value entered*

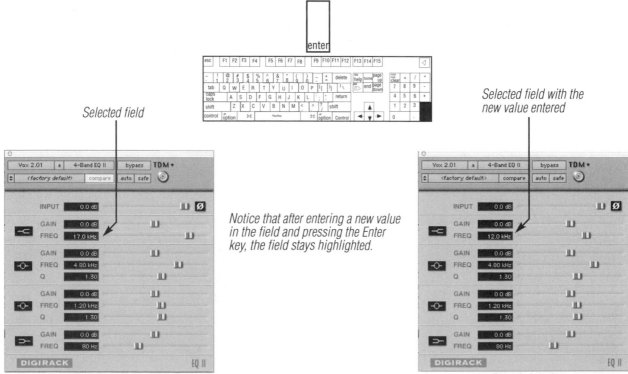

*Notice that after entering a new value
in the field and pressing the Enter
key, the field stays highlighted.*

Plug-in window　　　　　*Plug-in window*

Return (Alphanumeric Keypad)
PC: Enter

← **Enter Value and Exit Keyboard Entry mode**

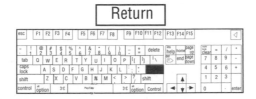

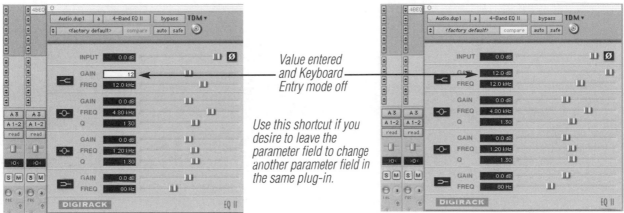

Value entered and Keyboard Entry mode off

Use this shortcut if you desire to leave the parameter field to change another parameter field in the same plug-in.

Plug-in window   *Plug-in window*

Type "k" after number to multiply by 1000
PC: Type "k" after number to multiply by 1000

← **For fields that support Kilohertz**

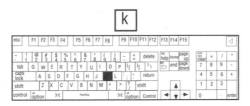

To apply this shortcut:
- Select the desired field to be changed.
- Type the desired number (value) followed by the letter "k."
- If you are finished with that specific parameter value, then press Return; if not, press Enter to continue experimenting with the parameter value.

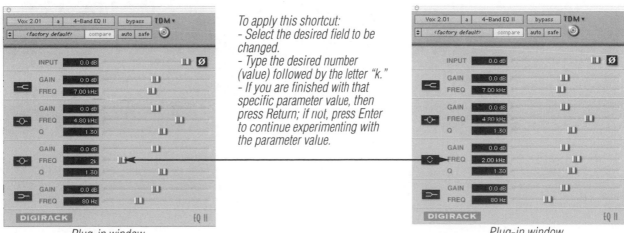

Plug-in window   *Plug-in window*

AUTOMATION

Leave absolute minimum/maximum breakpoints while trimming →

Shift + Trimming
PC: Shift + Trimming

Breakpoints

Notice that the highest breakpoints touching the top of the track remained in the same position after trimming the automation. The rest of the breakpoints were moved during trimming the automation.

Disable auto-creation of anchor breakpoints when trimming automation of a selection →

Option + Trimmer Tool
PC: Alt + Trimmer tool

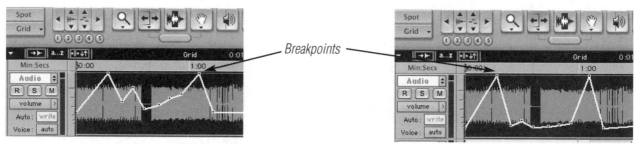

NOTE: Make sure you make a selection first before applying the shortcut.

Anchor breakpoints are created by default when trimming automation of a selection.

No anchor breakpoints are created when holding down the Option key. The anchor breakpoints moved along with the trimming amount by holding down the Option key while trimming the automation.

Control + Option + Command + Click on Parameters
(in plug-in window) **or track display format selector** (in edit window)

PC: Ctrl + Alt + Start + Click on Parameters (in plug-in window)
or track display format selector (in edit window)

← **Access Plug-in Automation Dialog**

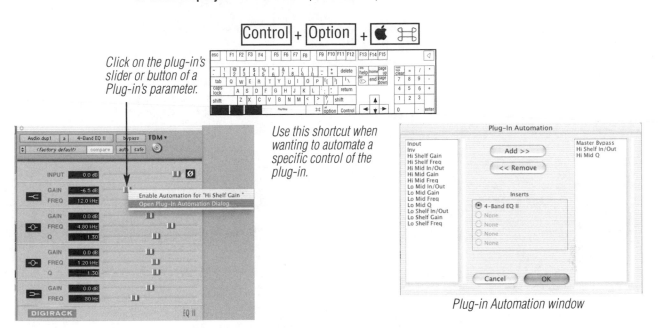

Click on the plug-in's slider or button of a Plug-in's parameter.

Use this shortcut when wanting to automate a specific control of the plug-in.

Plug-in Automation window

Command + Click on track display format selector
PC: Ctrl + Click on track display format selector

← **Disable/Enable Automation Playlist on selected track**

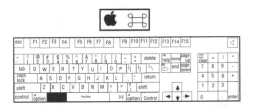

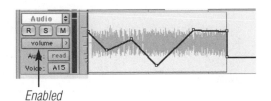

Enabled

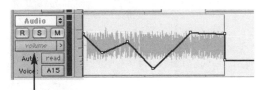

Disabled (button greyed out)

Apply this shortcut whenever you want to temporarily suspend the written automation on a specific track. You must do this for every track display format as desired. In other words, for "volume," you must do it in the "volume" track display format; for "mute," you must do it in the "mute" track display format, etc. Notice when you disable the automation, the button is greyed out.

Disable/Enable All Automation Playlists on Selected Track

→ Shift + Command + Click on track display format selector

PC: Ctrl + Shift + Click on track display format selector

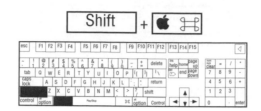

All automation playlists enabled

All automation playlists disabled

This disables all the track's automation parameters such as volume, mute, pan, etc., at once. Notice the disabled button is greyed out.

Vertically constrain automation movement

→ Shift + Move automation with Grabber

PC: Shift + Move automation with Grabber

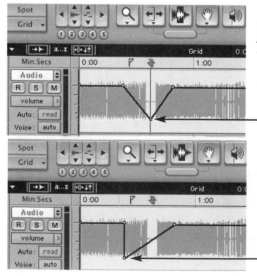

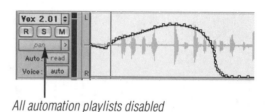

Use this shortcut to make sure you keep the breakpoint in a straight line while moving it.

You will only be able to move the breakpoint vertically.

The breakpoint was moved to the left because the Shift key was not held down while moving the breakpoint vertically.

Control + Command + V
PC: Start + Ctrl + V

← **<u>Special Paste of automation data between different controls</u>**

Nothing will happen if you only use Command + V; it must be Control + Command + V. Before you can paste the automation data, you must copy it with Control + Command + C.

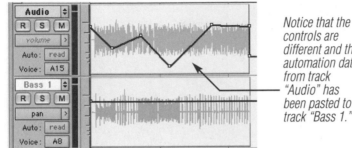

Notice that the controls are different and the automation data from track "Audio" has been pasted to track "Bass 1."

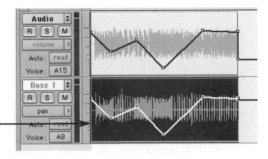

This shortcut allows you to paste, for example, volume automation to the pan control in the same track.

Control + Click on Transport's window End button
PC: Start + Click on Transport's window End button

← **<u>Write Automation to End of Session/Selection</u>**

(TDM systems only)

During playback.

For more details on how to use this function, refer to the section "Writing Automation to the Start, End or All of a Selection" in the Pro Tools Reference Guide (manual).

Transport window's End button

Control + Click on transport RTZ button
PC: Start + Click on transport RTZ button

← **<u>Write Automation to Start of Session/Selection</u>**

(TDM ystems only)

During playback.

For more details on how to use this function, refer to the section "Writing Automation to the Start, End or All of a Selection" in the Pro Tools Reference Guide (manual).

Transport window's RTZ button

Shift + Control + Click on transport End/RTZ button
PC: Start + Shift + Click or Shift + Right Mouse Click on transport End/RTZ button

← **<u>Write Automation from Start to End of Session/Selection</u>**

(TDM systems only)

During playback.

For more details on how to use this function, refer to the section "Writing Automation to the Start, End or All of a Selection" in the Pro Tools Reference Guide (manual).

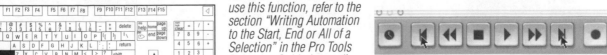

Copy to Send →

Option + Command + H *(TDM systems only)*
PC: Ctrl + Alt + H

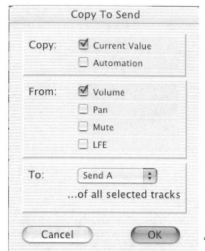

Use this shortcut to constantly update a headphone mix during an overdub session. You must select the name of the tracks you want to "Copy to Send," and then select the parameters, such as volume, pan, mute, etc.

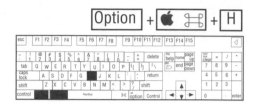

"Copy to Send" window

Display Automation Playlist of Automation-enabled control

→ Control + Option + Command + Click on control
PC: Ctrl + Right Mouse Click on control
Then choose to "Enable fader" or "Open plug-in automation" dialog.

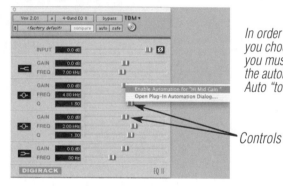

In order to automate the control you choose with this shortcut, you must set the track in any of the automation modes, such as Auto "touch," "latch," or "write."

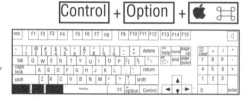

Controls

Scroll to & display track in default view in Edit window

→ Control + Command + Click on track name
in Mix, Edit, Inserts, or Sends window or Show/Hide Tracks List
PC: Right Mouse Click on track name
in Mix, Edit, Inserts, or Sends window or Show/Hide Tracks List

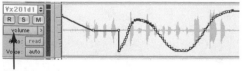

You can apply this shortcut by clicking on the track name in both Edit and Mix windows, Show/Hide list, and Insert window.

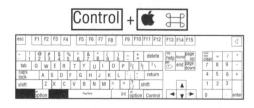

Volume track view

Waveform view. Notice the audio track view returned to its default view, the waveform.

Option + Command + T
PC: Ctrl + Alt + T

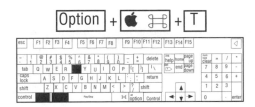

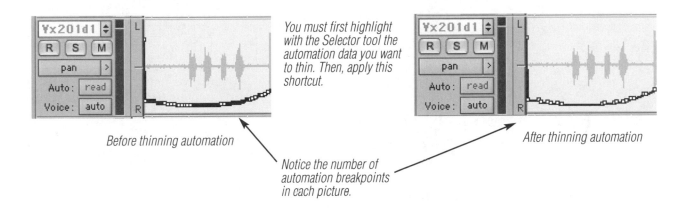

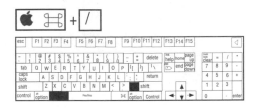

Before thinning automation

You must first highlight with the Selector tool the automation data you want to thin. Then, apply this shortcut.

Notice the number of automation breakpoints in each picture.

After thinning automation

Command + /
PC: Ctrl + 1

←**Write Automation to Current Parameters**

(TDM systems only)

Use this shortcut when you want to write snapshot automation over existing automation data on a particular parameter (vol, pan, mute, for example).

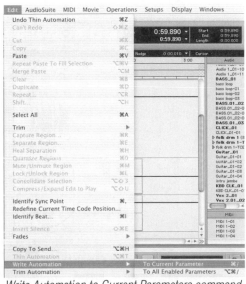

Write Automation to Current Parameters command

Write Automation to All ➤ Enabled Parameters

(TDM systems only)

Option + Command + /
PC: Ctrl + 1

Apply this shortcut when you want to write snapshot automation over existing automation data for all the automation parameters enabled in the "Automation Enabled" window.

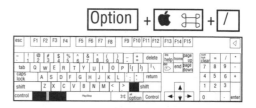

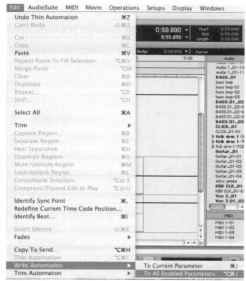

Write Automation to All Enabled Parameters command

Trim Automation to ➤ Current Parameters

(TDM systems only)

Shift + Command + /
PC: Ctrl + 1

This shortcut allows you to trim values as snapshots and apply the "relative" changes to the selected automation. This works in much the same way as the "Write Automation" command, except that it writes relative values instead of absolute values to automation data.

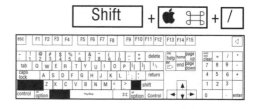

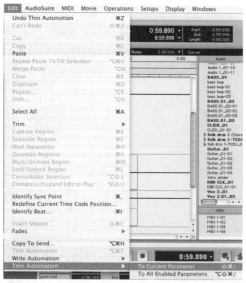

Trim Automation to Current Parameters command

Shift + Option + Command + / **← Trim Automation to All**
PC: Ctrl + 1   **Enabled Parameters**
                                      (TDM systems only)

This shortcut allows you to trim values as snapshots and apply the "relative" changes to the selected automation. This works in much the same way as the "Write Automation" command, except that it writes relative values instead of absolute values to automation data.

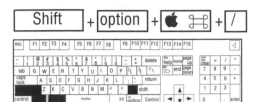

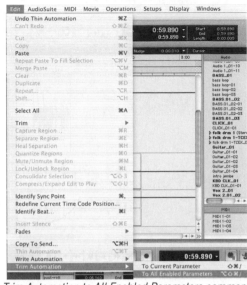

Trim Automation to All Enabled Parameters command

NOTE: When all tracks in selection are displaying automation playlists, hold down Control key during the following operations to affect all playlists on every track in the selection:

Delete Key **← Delete**
PC: Ctrl + Backspace

Command + D **← Duplicate**
PC: Ctrl + D

Command + B **← Clear**
PC: Ctrl + B

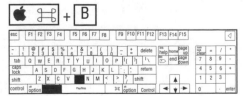

Command + X **← Cut**
PC: Ctrl + X

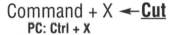

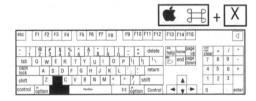

Command + C **← Copy**
PC: Ctrl + C

Shift + Command + E **← Insert Silence**
PC: Ctrl + Shift + E

COMMAND FOCUS MODE *For these one-key commands to work, the "a..z" button in the Edit window must be enabled.*

TDM systems only if using Pro Tools 5.x or lower; otherwise, these shortcuts work on TDM & LE 6.x systems.

<u>Zoom Level 1-5</u>

Alphanumeric Keys 1/2/3/4/5
PC: Alphanumeric Keys 1/2/3/4/5

This one-key command allows you to recall a horizontal zoom preset you stored by holding down the Command key (Ctrl for PC) and clicking on any of the five zoom preset buttons.

<u>Play to/from edit start by pre/post-roll value</u> →

Alphanumeric Keys 6 / 7
PC: Alphanumeric Keys 6 / 7

NOTE: You must enter a value on the pre/post roll fields for this shortcut to apply.

← *Playing to edit start by pre-roll value (4 bars)* →

You must make a region selection.

← *Playing from edit start by post-roll value (4 bars)* →

<u>Play to/from edit end by pre/post-roll amount</u> →

Alphanumeric Keys 8 / 9
PC: Alphanumeric Keys 8 / 9

NOTE: You must enter a value on the pre/post roll fields for this shortcut to apply.

← *Playing to edit end by pre-roll amount (4 bars)* →

You must make a region selection.

← *Playing from edit end by post-roll amount (4 bars)* →

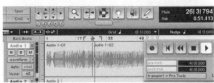

To accomplish this shortcut:
- *Disable the "Link Edit and Timeline Selection" function by clicking on the button to the right side of the "a..z" button.*
- *Make a selection in the Edit window.*
- *Press the "Ø" key on the alphanumeric keyboard.*
- *You will notice the Edit selection will be copied on the Timeline ruler.*

Alphanumeric Key Ø
PC: Alphanumeric Key Ø

← **Copy Edit Selection to Timeline Selection**

Timeline ruler

Edit Selection

"Linked Edit and Timeline Selection" button

To accomplish this one-key command:
- *Disable the "Link Edit and Timeline Selection" function by clicking on the button to the right side of the "a..z" button.*
- *Make a selection in the Timeline ruler.*
- *Press the "O" key on the alphanumeric keyboard.*
- *You will notice the Timeline selection will be copied on the Edit window.*

O
PC: O

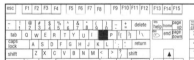

← **Copy Timeline Selection to Edit Selection**

Timeline Selection

Edit Selection

"Linked Edit and Timeline Selection" button

"-" Minus Key
PC: "-" Minus Key

← **Track View Toggle**

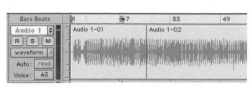

Waveform track view

This one-key command will toggle the track view between the "waveform" and "volume" views.

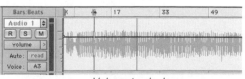

Volume track view

Capture Timecode →

"="

PC: "="

(On TDM systems and LE with DV Toolkit Option)
To capture timecode "on-the-fly," valid timecode must
be received by Pro Tools.

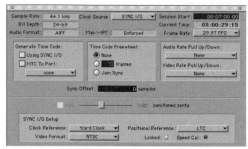

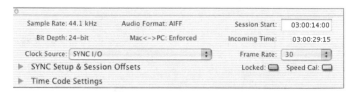

Session Setup window in Pro Tools 5.x   *Session Setup window in Pro Tools 6.x*

Center Timeline Start →

Q

PC: Q

This one-key command places the
start of a selected region in the
middle of the screen. You must
make a region selection first.

W
PC: W

← **Center Timeline End**

*This one-key command places
the end of a selected region in
the middle of the track. You must
make a region selection first.*

E
PC: E

← **Zoom Toggle**

- You must make a region selection first.
- Maximizes the selection view.

Zoom Out Horizontally →

R

PC: R

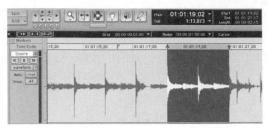 

NOTE: Pro Tools can be assigned to any Edit mode and any Edit tool to Zoom in/out vertically or horizontally for either audio or MIDI. In this example the "R" key was pressed three times. Notice the selected region was visually compressed.

Zoom In Horizontally →

T

PC: T

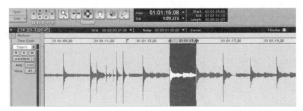 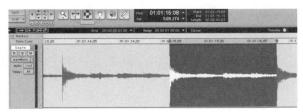

In this example the "T" key was pressed three times. Notice the selected region was visually expanded.

Snap Start (of selected region) to Timecode →

(Not available in Pro Tools LE)

Y

PC: Y

Snap Sync Point (of selected region) to Timecode

U
PC: U

- *You must have a Sync Point created.*
- *Does not work in Shuffle mode.*

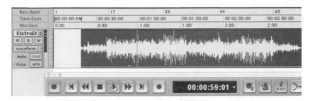

Snap End (of selected region) to Timecode

I
PC: I

(Not available in Pro Tools LE)
- *Does not work in Shuffle mode.*

Snap Start (of selected region) to Playhead

H
PC: H

You must have the "Continuous Scroll with Playhead" option enabled. This is located in Operations > Scroll Options.

Snap Sync Point (of selected → region) to Playhead

J

PC: J

You must have the "Continuous Scroll with Playhead" option enabled. This is located in Operations > Scroll Options.

You must create a Sync point by using "Identify Sync point" in the Edit menu.

Sync point

Sync point

Snap End (of selected → region) to Playhead

Does not work in Shuffle mode.

K

PC: K

Move Edit Selection Up →

P

PC: P

The "P" key was pressed once.

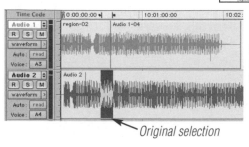

You can move up the cursor from one track to another, or a region selection, as in this example.

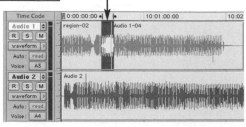

Original selection

";" (Semicolon)
PC: ";" (Semicolon)

← **Move Edit Selection Down**

Original selection

You can move down the cursor or selection as many times as you desire.

Notice the selection moved down twice by pressing the ";" key two times.

L
PC: L

← **Tab Back**

You must enable the "Tab to Transient" function.
You can either move the cursor only or move a selection.

Region selection was expanded to the left by clicking on the "L" key twice while holding down the Shift key.

Region selected with the "Tab to Transient" funtion.

" ' " (Apostrophe)
PC: ' (Apostrophe)

← **Tab Forward**

You must enable the "Tab to Transient" function.
You can either move the cursor only or expand a region selection.

Original selection

Notice the region selection was expanded to the right by pressing the " ' " key twice while holding down the Shift key.

Play Timeline Selection →

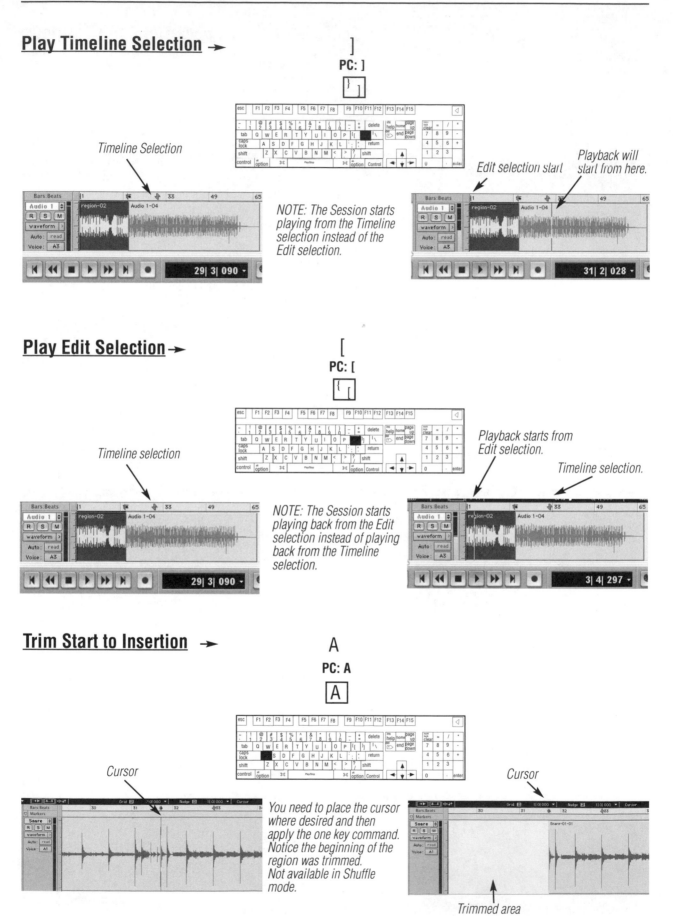

PC:]

Timeline Selection

Edit selection start

Playback will start from here.

NOTE: The Session starts playing from the Timeline selection instead of the Edit selection.

29| 3| 090 ·

31| 2| 028 ·

Play Edit Selection →

PC: [

Timeline selection

Playback starts from Edit selection.

Timeline selection.

NOTE: The Session starts playing back from the Edit selection instead of playing back from the Timeline selection.

29| 3| 090 ·

3| 4| 297 ·

Trim Start to Insertion →

A

PC: A

Cursor

Cursor

You need to place the cursor where desired and then apply the one key command. Notice the beginning of the region was trimmed. Not available in Shuffle mode.

Trimmed area

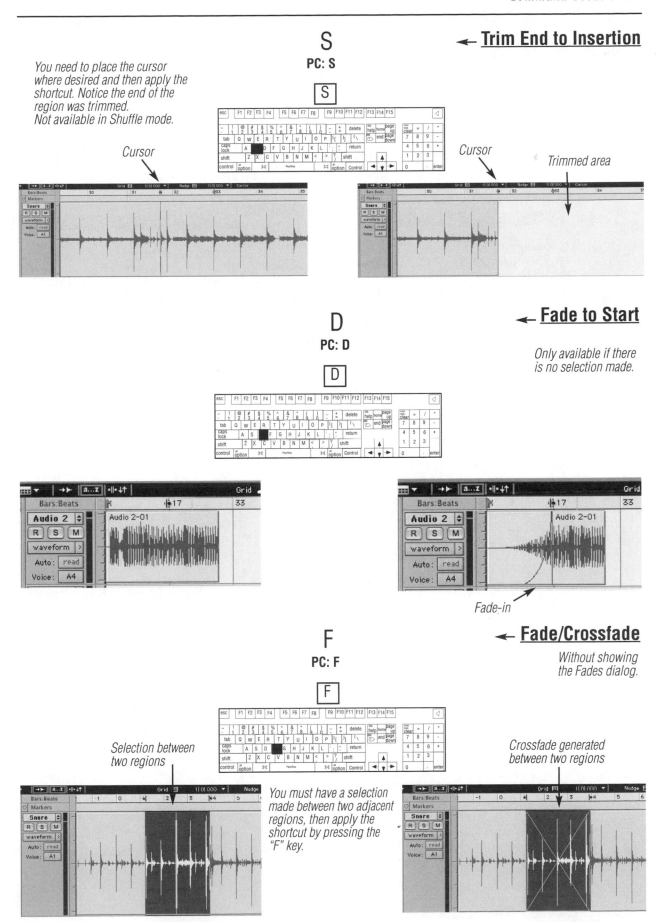

S

PC: S

← Trim End to Insertion

You need to place the cursor where desired and then apply the shortcut. Notice the end of the region was trimmed.
Not available in Shuffle mode.

Cursor

Cursor

Trimmed area

D

PC: D

← Fade to Start

Only available if there is no selection made.

Fade-in

F

PC: F

← Fade/Crossfade

Without showing the Fades dialog.

Selection between two regions

Crossfade generated between two regions

You must have a selection made between two adjacent regions, then apply the shortcut by pressing the "F" key.

Fade to End →

*Only available if there
is no selection made.*

G

PC: G

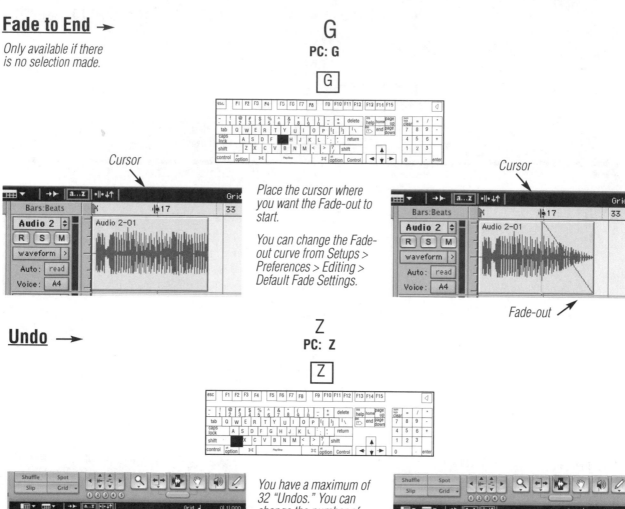

Cursor

*Place the cursor where
you want the Fade-out to
start.*

*You can change the Fade-
out curve from Setups >
Preferences > Editing >
Default Fade Settings.*

Cursor

Fade-out →

Undo →

Z

PC: Z

*You have a maximum of
32 "Undos." You can
change the number of
Undos from Setups >
Preferences > Editing >
Levels of Undo.*

Region deleted →

The region re-appeared →
by pressing the "Z" key.

Cut →

X

PC: X

*You must first make a
region selection to use this
one-key command.*

C

PC: C

To copy a region, you must select it first and then press the "C" key.

← **<u>Copy</u>**

V

PC: V

Before applying the Paste command, place the cursor wherever you want the copied region to be pasted.

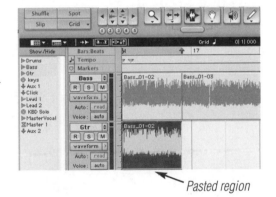

← **<u>Paste</u>**

Pasted region

B

PC: B

← **<u>Separate</u>**

Making a region selection to be separated

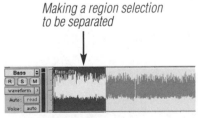

The new region shows the name given by you in the previous step.

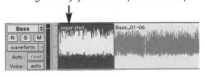

If you place the cursor anywhere in a region and then press the "B" key, the region will be separated without asking you to rename it.

If you make a region selection to separate it from the entire region, Pro Tools will prompt you to rename the newly separated region. It won't prompt you for a new name if the "Auto-name Separated Region" option is enabled in the Setups > Preferences > Editing menu.

Timeline Insertion Follows Playback →

N

PC: N

In this example, the "Timeline Insertion Follows Playback" option is disabled. This means every time you press Play or the Spacebar, the Playback will start from the same place.

In this example, the "Timeline Insertion Follows Playback" option is enabled. Every time you press Play or the Spacebar, the Playback will start from where the last playback stopped.

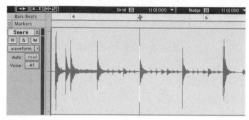

You can also enable and disable the "Timeline Insertion Follows Playback" option in the Setups > Preferences > Operation menu.

Original playback location

New playback start location with the "Timeline Insertion Follows Playback" option enabled.

Nudge Back by Next Nudge Value →

M

PC: M

You can nudge selections, or just the cursor itself.

You must select the proper Nudge interval as desired.

Nudge interval selection

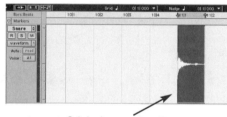

This one-key command will move the cursor or region by the next larger value in the "Nudge" pop-up menu. Example: If the Nudge value is set to eighth-notes, and you want to nudge by a larger value, you can nudge it to the next larger value, or quarter-notes.

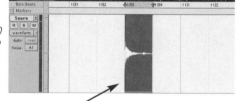

Original cursor location

Notice the cursor moved one half-note interval to the left, since the nudge interval was set to a quarter-note value.

Nudge Back by Nudge Value →

<

PC: <

Original position (11 | 1 | 000)

Current Nudge value selector

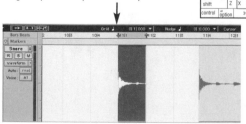

This one-key command moves the cursor or selected region to the left by the current Nudge value interval.

The region was moved to the left by a quarter-note interval (10|4|000).

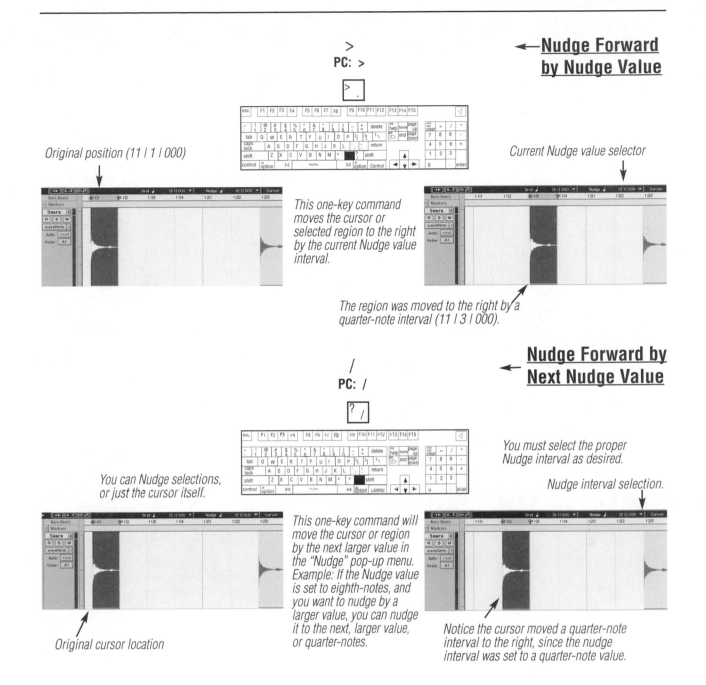

← Nudge Forward by Nudge Value

>
PC: >

Original position (11 / 1 / 000)

This one-key command moves the cursor or selected region to the right by the current Nudge value interval.

Current Nudge value selector

The region was moved to the right by a quarter-note interval (11 / 3 / 000).

Nudge Forward by Next Nudge Value ←

/
PC: /

You can Nudge selections, or just the cursor itself.

You must select the proper Nudge interval as desired.

Nudge interval selection.

This one-key command will move the cursor or region by the next larger value in the "Nudge" pop-up menu. Example: If the Nudge value is set to eighth-notes, and you want to nudge by a larger value, you can nudge it to the next, larger value, or quarter-notes.

Original cursor location

Notice the cursor moved a quarter-note interval to the right, since the nudge interval was set to a quarter-note value.

Acknowledgments

I would like to express my thanks and appreciation to those who collaborated with me on this book, and to all my friends and family who patiently supported me and helped me in one way or another throughout the completion of this important project.

First of all, to my wife, Marina Zapata Valenzuela, for her patience and understanding, and for believing in me and the project. Secondly, to Matt Kelsey, Publisher of Backbeat Books, for giving me the opportunity to publish this book and for his patience. Thanks, Matt. To my right hand, Ana Lorente Izquierdo, for her invaluable time, talent, effort, and persistence.

To the AudioGraph International team: Ma. del Refugio Valenzuela, Andre Oliveira, George Madaraz, Debbie Green, Luis Alberto Capilla, Oscar Elizondo, Gary Glass, Neal Kiyoshi Fujio, Giovanna Imbesi, Abel Chen, Hillary Beth, Don Quentin Hannah, Vivian Khor, Severine Baron, Jamie Steele, and Roberto C. González Fócil.

To Backbeat Books: Nancy Tabor, Karl Coryat, Richard Johnston, Amy Miller, Kevin Becketti, Nina Lesowitz, and the late Jay Kahn.

To Digidesign: Christopher Bock, Paul Floecker, Sirpa King, Claudia Cursio, Mary Stevens, Andy Cook, Jon Connolly, Victoria Faveau, Mark Kirshner, Boe Gatiss, Dusty DiMercurio, Bill Lackey, Jerry Antonelli, Alex Steinhart, José "Pepe" Reveles, Adinaldo Neves, and Felipe Capilla.

Thanks to all of you!
Chilitos

About the Author

José "Chilitos" Valenzuela is a recording, mixing, electronic music, and computer engineer born in Tijuana, B. C., Mexico. He graduated in Audio, Electronic Music and Computer Science Engineering from Baja California's Institute of Technology (ITR #21), California State University Dominguez Hills in Carson, CA, and UCLA.

Valenzuela has worked as an audio engineer for Oberheim Electronics (a synthesizer manufacturer) and for the ABC TV Network during the 1984 Olympic Games held in Los Angeles, CA. He also worked as design engineer for Fast Forward Designs (now Line 6) where he collaborated in the design of several Alesis Corp. and Digidesign products, among others.

As a recording, mixing, and mastering engineer, Valenzuela has worked for internationally renowned artists and producers such as Whitney Houston, Elton John, The Go-Go's, Jay Graydon, Alejandro Lerner, Keith Emerson, Pepe Aguilar, Marcelo Cezán, John Waite (The Babys), and Michael Sembello, among others.

In the post-production world, Valenzuela has worked as a sound-effects designer and synthesizer programmer in feature films such as *Star Trek: Generations*, *Dark Devil*, and others.

He has been the editor of *Guitar Player* magazine's Spanish edition, editorial director of *Latin GRAMMY* magazine, and collaborator of *Mix* magazine's Spanish edition.

In addition to writing several books, Valenzuela has given professional audio conferences in the United States, Spain, and several countries in Latin America.

Valenzuela is a UCLA Professor, Pro Tools consultant, and President of Audio-Graph International, which is a Spanish Information Center for Music and Technology, and a training center certified by Digidesign for Pro Tools in English and Spanish.

Valenzuela has started a music production company in Los Angeles, where he will develop and produce new and already established Latin and American artists, in both English and Spanish.

WHEN IT COMES TO MAKING MUSIC, WE WROTE THE BOOK.

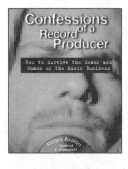